The Hebrew Verbless Clause
in the Pentateuch

Francis I. Andersen

Journal of Biblical Literature
Monograph Series XIV

Robert A. Kraft, Editor

Published for the
Society of Biblical Literature

by
Abingdon Press

Nashville   New York

THE HEBREW VERBLESS CLAUSE IN THE PENTATEUCH

Standard Book Number: 687-20628-6
Library of Congress Catalog Card Number: 78-97574

SET UP, PRINTED, AND BOUND BY THE
PARTHENON PRESS, AT NASHVILLE,
TENNESSEE, UNITED STATES OF AMERICA

Preface

This study owes so much to so many persons that it is impossible to thank them all. Dr. W. F. Albright has offered ceaseless encourage-ment and many discussions. Linguistic stimulus, not to say provoca-tion, has come from Dr. T. O. Lambdin (Harvard) and Dr. Kenneth L. Pike (University of Michigan). The ideas of Robert E. Longacre have given impetus to the work from the beginning. Other members of the Summer Institute of Linguistics have helped keep it moving, especially Dr. Harland B. Kerr and his wife, Marie, whose dedication of scientific skill and Christian compassion to the Wiru people of New Guinea has been a constant inspiration.

Through it all my wife, Lois, has never failed to support and en-courage me. All that love and gratitude can express belongs to her.

Contents

9

IV: Tables

11

The Transliteration of Hebrew

The system of transliteration used here is a normalized quasi-phonemic representation of the Masoretic conventional orthography. Variations in spelling due to inconsistencies in the use of *matres lectionis* have been ignored. All long vowels are represented as $\bar{v}$, no matter what their history; for example, long *o* is *ō* whether $<*u$, $<*aw$, $<*â$, and whether spelled with or without a *mater lectionis*. The *matres lectionis* are not transcribed as consonants; for example, *ze*, not *zeh*, "this." Doubling of consonants is shown, but spirantization of stops is ignored as subphonemic. The conventional equivalents of the consonants are used.

Table of Abbreviations and Glossary
of Some Linguistic Terms

#	designates a clause type in the Corpus (Part III)
+	Obligatory constituent
±	Optional constituent
--->	Rewrite as, generates
/	indicates that the tagmemes are not necessarily manifested in the sequence written
(X,Y,Z, ...)	Any one, but only one, of the items may be selected
X,Y,Z, ...	Any number of items may be selected
\<X–Y\>	Syntagmeme relating X and Y (sometimes X–Y)
\<Z\>	Syntagmemic relationship Z
X... ...X	Discontinuous manifestation of tagmeme X
SSus,SRes	The comma indicates resumption after *casus pendens*
Ø	A zero tagma; absence of overt manifestation of a tagmeme exponent is a contrastive signal
A	Apposition

Adn	Adnominal relator
Adv	Adverb
Allosyntagma	Predictable (contextually conditioned) variant manifestation of a syntagmeme
C	Coordination; the "Book of the Covenant" as a source
Cj	Conjunction
Cl	Clause
Co	Coordinating conjunction, coordinated clause
Core	Maximal form of a clause without its margins
Ct	Construct relationship
D	Used in the Corpus to identify the putative deuteronomic source but not usually in Deuteronomy itself
E	Used in the Corpus to identify the putative elohistic source
Endocentric	A construction whose distribution is the same as that of one of its constituents
Eq	Equivalent (in function)
Exc	Exclamation
Exocentric	A construction that is not endocentric
Exponent	A form that manifests a function
H	Used in the Corpus to identify the "Holiness Code" as a source
If	Infinitive
Ind	Independent; a clause that is a sentence
Int	Interrogative
J	Used in the Corpus to identify the putative yahwistic source
JPS	Jewish Publication Society *Torah*
KJV	The King James Version of the Bible
L	A locational modifier; in the Corpus it identifies the putative "Lay" source
LXX	Septuagint
M	Modification
Md	Modifier
Mg	Clause-marginal tagmeme; marginal reading
MT	Masoretic text. Biblical references herein are based on MT.
N	Noun
Nd	Definite noun (Article + Noun)
Neg	Negator

Ni	Indefinite noun
Nom	Nominalizer; nominalized construction
Np	Proper noun (person or place name)
Ns	Suffixed noun (Noun + Pronoun-suffix)
Nucleus	Minimal manifestation of syntagmeme of predication
Num	Numeral (phrase)
Numd	Definite numeral (phrase)
Numi	Indefinite numeral
P	Predicate; used in the Corpus to identify the putative priestly source
Parameter	A structural feature that may be kept constant so as to control the study of concomitant variables
Part	Partitive phrase (*min-* + Noun)
Ph	Phrase
Pp	Preposition
Pr	Pronoun
Pt	Participle
Ptd	Definite participle (Article + Participle)
Pti	Indefinite participle
Re	Interclause relator
Res	Resumptive
RSV	Revised Standard Version of the Bible, 1952
S	Subject
s	Suffix
Se	Sentence
Sub	Subordinating conjunction; subordinated clause
Sus	Suspended subject, *casus pendens*
Syntagmeme	The minimal integral unit of grammatical relationship
Tagmeme	A function-set correlation in grammatical structure
Transformation	An operation that exhibits "deep" grammatical relationships between two constructions
Voc	Vocative

Part I

Orientation

1. Previous Study of the Verbless Clause

The grammar of the verbless clause, traditionally called the nominal sentence, in biblical Hebrew was stated by C. Albrecht.[1] The typical presentation in Gesenius' *Grammar* is a summary of Albrecht's conclusions.[2] More recently Carl Brockelmann[3] and Ronald J. Williams[4] have devoted about one page to the topic of word sequence in the nominal sentence, repeating accepted results. The sequence *subject-predicate* is said to be normal. Exceptions in which S follows P are explained by saying that P is put first as the dominant idea or as the psychological subject of the sentence or for emphasis.

Such concepts are really exegetical inferences and not grammatical categories. As a result, many grammars make misleading statements about the structure of the verbless clause in Hebrew. Paul Auvray includes as exercises in his grammar thirty clauses like *haddābār ṭōb*, "the word is good," with no hint of an alternate possibility.[5] Yet out of nearly two thousand verbless clauses in the Pentateuch not one has this structure. (See #112.) It is true that a few may be found like *wᵉhabbōr rēq*, "and the pit is empty" (Gen. 37:24). But here the use of the conjunction together with the sequence <S–P> gives the clause a special circumstantial function in relation to neighboring clauses. (See Rule 5, p. 45.) Such a clause is not a model for independent clauses. The Pentateuch affords only one clause that resembles Auvray's example: *haggal hazze ʿēd bēnī ūbēnᵉkā hayyōm*, "this heap is a witness between me and you today" (Gen. 31:48). Its uniqueness invites a different explanation. Either the sentence is precative, or the predicate is a participle (Rule 7, p. 47).

Samuel G. Green has a brief observation that "the predicate is often placed first,"[6] but his illustrations all have the sequence S–P.[7] R. Laird Harris' only remark about the verbless clause is to supply as illustration *šēt bēn*, "Seth is a son."[8] If such a clause was acceptable in classical Hebrew, it was rare. The Pentateuch contains only three possible examples, each of which has its difficulty. (See the detailed discussion under Rule 3, p. 42.)

James Kennedy's discussion, though brief, is nearer the mark, since he recognizes that a predicate noun or adjective usually comes first (Rule 3, p. 42). He is also aware of the occurrence of discontinuous predicates.[9] This important sequence P–S for predicate adjective had already been noted in Rödiger's version of Gesenius' *Grammar*, with the explanation that the predicate is "the most important member of the sentence."[10] A. B. Davidson's teaching was less clear. He maintained that an indefinite predicate adjective may come before or after the noun subject, usually before.[11] J. Weingreen suggests that P–S and S–P are equally possible, the word coming first being the one emphasized.[12]

This sampling of opinion should be enough to show that existing descriptions of the verbless clause in biblical Hebrew are unsatisfactory. They are uncertain as to what are normal patterns. Explanations of exceptions to the supposed rule S–P are often given in terms of concepts like *emphasis* or *importance*, which have no empirical status. Another flaw in the method is attempted proof by illustrations, some of which cannot be found in real texts at all.

2. The Present Investigation

The purpose of the present study is to remedy this lack by an exhaustive survey of the verbless clauses in the Pentateuch. Contemporary linguistic method is used, although space does not allow complete description of the theory involved nor rigorous definition of all terms used. In any event, many good discussions of modern linguistics are available.[1] The facts are the same, no matter what theoretical model is used to interpret them; so the facts are given prominence in this monograph.

After some criticism of previous work (pp. 20-24), there is an introduction to some linguistic concepts that have guided the present research (pp. 25-27). Here also the main structural variables of the verbless clause are identified, and the salient questions are stated (pp. 24-25).

Thus it is possible to formulate a set of rules for describing all the kinds of verbless clauses which are possible in Hebrew. Here terminology is defined, and symbols for grammatical units are introduced (pp. 27-30). The result is a calculus for generating all the verbless clauses actually found in the sources, as well as unattested clauses of identical construction, which presumably would also be acceptable to native speakers as "grammatical."

Since all formal distinctions may have grammatical significance, it is essential that all operating concepts be defined precisely and adhered to strictly. This makes it difficult to organize the vast body of data so that no detail is neglected. To marshal all the evidence in an orderly way, the full repertoire of clause types, involving hundreds of distinct patterns, is set out in the Corpus (Part III), with representative examples and full references. The arrangement of the Corpus is shown in the Contents (pp. 5-12). Data from the Corpus are summarized in Tables (Part IV, see pp. 109-20).

Description of these data proceeds by successive approximations. The first stage is represented by the general scheme outlined on pages 31-39. This is a broad provisional induction covering all possibilities. In the light of the statistics in Part IV, it is possible to describe some patterns as common, others as rare.

Sometimes the same parts of speech occur in the same relationship in clauses with more than one pattern. For example, a pronoun as subject with an indefinite noun as predicate occurs in either sequence S–P (#24) or P–S (#94). The first is rare; the second is common. The pattern which occurs more frequently will be considered normal. Such a fact may be stated in the form of a rule (pp. 39-50).

The less common alternate sequence may be inexplicable, that is, exceptional. But since languages tend to be economical in the use of all available contrasts, it is more likely that the alternate sequence is part of the signal of a different function for the clause. For the present example, while sequence P–S is normal for independent clauses (#94 in contrast with #24), sequence S–P is preferred for circumstantial clauses (#187 in contrast with #282); sequence S–P signals the circumstantial function of the clause.

The study proceeds in stages. At first only the simplest kinds of clauses are considered, namely those with a simple subject and a simple predicate and no other items, such as adverbs or conjunctions. By restricting the inquiry further to clauses with the same kind of subject (a pronoun), two sequences are found: subject followed by predicate (S–P) and predicate followed by subject (P–S). The sequence depends on the kind of predicate used. This leads to the recognition of two types of clause: the clause which identifies the subject and the clause which classifies the subject (pp. 31-34).

From this first stage it is then possible to advance to more complex questions. The full range of possible subjects is brought in, and the initial conclusions are confirmed (pp. 33-35). The picture is enlarged further by including more complicated clauses, some of which have discontinuity in the subject or the predicate or both (pp. 36-37). Finally, clauses which express a wish (precative) or ask a question (interrogative) are treated (pp. 38-39). This completes the discovery of normal patterns.

The data are then reviewed again with special attention to the various kinds of predicate (pp. 39-50). This allows the normal patterns to be described in more detail, in the form of rules. In the light of these rules, apparent exceptions can be examined, leading to a closer study of selected problems (for example, p. 43).

3. Criticism of Previous Work

The study of the nominal sentence by Albrecht [1] has been accepted as standard for many years; but it is open to some theoretical and methodological objections.

1. No proper foundation is laid for the study of clause or sentence structure. Without working definitions of these linguistic units, criteria are lacking for the identification and isolation of appropriate data. For example, Brockelmann uses Jer. 24:2 as an illustration; [2] but this is not a clause. It is part of a distributive object in apposition with a preceding noun. Ezek. 41:22 is another example used in the same place, as also by Joüon. [3] Yet RSV shows that this is probably not a sentence, although it is easily transformed into one in translation. It belongs to a special category of discourse, common in the priestly materials, in which specifications and dimensions are prescribed. In any case, such clauses cannot be taken as paradigms for normal syntax.

It must be admitted that, in spite of constant discussion, no foolproof definition of *sentence* has been achieved in theoretical linguistics. [4] For present purposes it is advantageous to distinguish *clause* and *sentence*. [5] A clause is a construction in which the syntagmeme of predication is manifested once. It should be added that a clause may include another clause or be itself part of a larger clause. [6] For example, a clause may be the object of a verb and so part of the predicate of the clause containing that verb. So long as levels of structure are distinguished, such constructions do not conflict with the definition: the syntagmeme of predication is manifested only once in each clause-level construction.

A sentence is a grammatically self-contained construction. [7] The grammatical functions of all constituents in a sentence may be described in terms of relationships to other constitutents in the same sentence. This definition is operational; it falls short of theoretical rigor. Few sentences are as completely isolated as the definition requires. Most stand in extended relationships to their context, verbal or nonverbal. But expansion of the frame of reference to paragraph structure and discourse analysis is not possible here.

2. In order to talk about the sequence of subject (S) and predicate (P) in a clause, it is essential that these core constituents be identified

and distinguished as certainly as possible. This is a vexed question whose uncertainty at the outset haunts all the subsequent analysis. Albrecht gave no attention to this problem; so there is scope for disagreement. What he identifies as S may often be considered as P.

A quasi-semantic definition of a clause (simple sentence) as the linguistic expression of a proposition that combines a subject of discourse with a statement about this subject [8] is heuristically inadequate. In some clauses the logical topic may not be the grammatical subject; for example, the traditional *casus pendens*. In one sense, everything that is said is part of the subject matter; and everything that is said, including the announcement of the topic, is information about the subject. While recourse to meaning for analysis cannot be entirely avoided, at this point provisional identifications can be secured by the simultaneous use of both formal and semantic clues. In the first stages S may be identified when its correspondence to something in the preceding discourse shows it to be the continuing topic of discourse. Examples are found in Isa. 5:7 and 6:13, where this consideration shows that the literal RSV translation has missed the chiasmus and confused S and P. The referential use of a pronoun or of the article often serves as a clue to S. The matching rule that P is indefinite in relationship to S is of some use; but these tests fail when both core constituents are definite.

The distinction between S and P is established with some certainty when a statement is made in answer to a question: the topic has already been mentioned in the question; new information emerges as the P of the answer.[9] But this approach does not work with an interrogative clause itself; a question is not a proposition to be analyzed as *topic* plus *comment*. But since P in the response replaces the interrogative constituent in the question, at least when the question is a request for information,[10] the interrogative tagmeme may be identified as P in a question clause.[11] Because of these special problems, it is best to deal with interrogative clauses separately instead of mixing them with indicative statements as Albrecht does.

3. In Albrecht's study eight categories of nominal sentence were distinguished, depending on whether the predicate was (A) a substantive, (B) an adjective, (C) a participle, (D) an adverb, (E) a prepositional construction, (F) an infinitive, (G) a numeral, (H) a pronoun. The categories are not defined; but it cannot be taken for granted that these distinctions are obvious. For example, the structure of the verbless clause in Hebrew does not seem to make any formal distinctions between what have been traditionally called nouns and adjectives. The insight of Plato, who placed verbs and adjectives

together in the same class as predicators, illustrates the problem further. How does one decide whether *qērēḥ hū'* (Lev. 13:40) means "he is bald" (adjective) or "he is a bald man" (noun)?

Again, the partitive use of *min*, "from," results in a prepositional phrase with substantive meaning; for example, *miyyaldē hā'ibrīm ze*, "this is (one) of the Hebrew boys" (Exod. 2:6; #99).[12] Should such a phrase be called a noun? Another example of this kind of arbitrariness is seen in Albrecht's listing of many prepositional phrases (his category E) as adverbs (his category D).

In the present study there is recognition of eighteen categories of constituent, formally defined, that may be the S or P of a verbless clause. Interrogatives constitute an additional class (Table 1).

4. When classification of clause types is based only on the kind of predicate, this assumes that it does not make any difference what the subject is. This should not be taken for granted; it should be demonstrated. Instead of following Albrecht's method of treating all subjects alike, the present study uses the same eighteen categories of constituent to describe verbless clauses with reference to both S and P.

5. While Albrecht made a distinction between *substantive* and *adjective* that may be unreal, there are important distinctions among substantives that should not be overlooked. This includes the problem of the grammatical status of numerals, participles, and infinitives as substantives. By distinguishing between proper nouns, definite nouns, suffixed nouns, and indefinite nouns, the question of the grammatical function of definiteness is raised. Albrecht gave this no consideration at all; but the results given below indicate that definiteness is the key to understanding the structures of verbless clauses in Hebrew.

6. It should not be assumed that all verbless clauses belong to the same grammatical set. It will be shown below that predication by means of participles is verbal rather than nominal in character. Clauses containing numerals occur in the Pentateuch as statements of the results of a census or of the specifications of a building. Their special patterns may be dialectal or stylistic within the priestly tradition; but in any case they call for special attention.

7. It is not sufficient to discuss only S and P, ignoring other constituents, whether modifiers of S or P or modifiers of the clause as a whole. Perturbation of normal structure by the presence of additional items may call for recognition. This was not allowed for in Albrecht's broad generalizations from all kinds of clauses, nor called in as an explanation of exceptions. An example is afforded by nominalized verbless clauses in which the P is negated. There are 242 nominalized verbless clauses in the Pentateuch. The sequence S–P is found in

209 of these, none of which has a negated P. The five clauses with negation have the less usual sequence P–S.[13]

Albrecht did suggest, however, that an abnormal sequence could arise when a constituent was long. In this he was only partly correct, since a long S or P more frequently gives rise to discontinuity than to dislocation.

8. This phenomenon of discontinuity requires special attention, since it complicates the question of sequence. For example, when a phrase used as P is broken by the intrusion of S, the pattern is P...S ...P. It is then necessary to distinguish the nucleus within this core construction, that is, the minimum manifestation of the S/P syntagmeme. See p. 29.

9. The place and function of a clause in wider discourse is another problem overlooked by Albrecht. Internal structure may be correlated with and so presumably is part of the signal of external function. Albrecht ignored conjunctions and other connecting signals, as if it made no difference whether a clause was independent, circumstantial, parenthetical, coordinate, subordinate, or relative. In addition to such grammatical relationships with the linguistic context, clauses may have different behavioral functions in discourse. For example, a study of paragraph structure may clarify the syntax of glosses, headings, colophons, lists; and attention to cultural conventions in speech may elucidate the status of propositions, wishes, commands, prescriptions, questions.

A specific example will illustrate this problem. Oskar Grether quotes *zăhab hā'āreṣ hahi' ṭōb,* "the gold of that land is good" (Gen. 2:12a) as an illustration of the allegedly normal sequence S–P. But the majority of independent declarative verbless clauses with such constituents have the sequence P–S (Rule 3, p. 42). The example is not germane, because the conjunction *w–* has been left out. In contrast to P–S for an independent clause, S–P is normal for such a circumstantial clause. But it is mischievous to misquote a coordinated clause as evidence of the structure of a noncoordinated clause.[14]

10. Besides verbal and verbless clauses, Hebrew has a class of clause in which predication is manifested by such quasi verbals as *yēš, 'ōd, hinnē,* etc. These in turn are related to clauses using an equative verb. Albrecht did not discuss the role of words like *hinnē,* even though they occur in some of his examples. Quasi-verbal clauses need to be separated from verbless ones, even though they are interrelated by important transformations. This research is not included in the present monograph.

11. Albrecht was aware that considerations of prosody may some-

times explain an apparently anomalous sequence; for example, a poetic requirement of chiasmus may reverse the usual pattern. Compare Isa. 5:7. Most poetry was excluded from Albrecht's data. The poetry of the Pentateuch here reveals some interesting problems, but the sample is small. A full study of the syntax of poetry is called for.

12. Having laid down the sequence S–P as normative, Albrecht and others tend to make their chief explanation of numerous examples of P–S an alleged emphasis on P. No grammatical basis for such an interpretation is secured by, say, setting such clauses in contrast with otherwise identical clauses in which there is no such emphasis, or by reference to the linguistic environment that shows why such supposed emphasis is appropriate.

The appeal to *emphasis* is not consistent. The P–S sequence of [*kî*] *hōle hū'* "[for] he is sick," at I Sam. 19:14 is explained by emphasis on P; but at I Kings 14:5 the same construction is said to be possible because S is a pronoun.[15]

13. The indiscriminate application of inductive method to the entire text of the Old Testament supposes that the corpus is linguistically homogeneous. This should not be assumed. According to critical theory, which the present writer views with great skepticism, the materials in the Pentateuch are drawn from widely differing times, localities, and traditions. Should there be dialectal or historical contrasts in the patterns of verbless clauses, these may show up in the consistent distribution of contrasting patterns in the several putative sources. So that this possibility may be studied, the commonly accepted sources are indicated in the Corpus along with the references.[16]

4. The Components of the Problem

This critical review opens the way for a statement of eight distinct questions about the structure and function of verbless clauses. These questions lead to the classification of all the clause types that are found.

1. What is the function of the clause in discourse? Three functions are distinguished: declarative, precative, interrogative. It is possible that a fourth function—prescriptive—might be established by better methods of discourse analysis. But since the present study is mainly concerned with inner structure, at this stage prescriptive clauses are not distinguished from declarative, although they might in some respects be considered precative.

Three kinds of interrogation may be distinguished: a request for identification or classification, using interrogatives *mî* or *ma-;* a request for corroboration, using *hă-;* a request for information, using *'ānā,* "whither?"; *'ēpō',* "where?"; *mē'ayin,* "whence?"; *lāmmā, maddū',* "why?"

2. What is the grammatical function of the clause in its linguistic context? Four relationships are distinguished: independent, coordinate, subordinate, nominalized. More detailed investigation of interclause relationships, outside the scope of the present study, should make it possible to distinguish three kinds of coordination: circumstantial, conjunctive, disjunctive.

Questions 1 and 2 lead to the identification of three sets and eight subsets of clauses. (Only declarative clauses are Sub or Nom.) These are assembled in the eight subsections of the Corpus. Their statistics are shown in Tables 7-15.

3. Does the clause have any marginal modifiers? Clauses with margins are listed separately in the Corpus.

4. What is the nuclear structure of the clause? There are two possibilities: S–P and P–S. Hence each subsection in the Corpus has two sub-subsections.

5. Does the clause have *casus pendens* with resumptive subject? (See ##84-88.)

6. Is there discontinuity in S or P or both?

Questions 5 and 6 lead to the identification of thirteen different clause cores (Table 2).

7. What is the form category of the subject?

8. What is the form category of the predicate?

Questions 7 and 8 lead to the identification of eighteen categories of S or P (Table 1).

If all theoretical possibilities were realized, there would be 33,696 kinds of declarative verbless clauses. The Corpus shows that more than four hundred of these patterns are manifested in the Pentateuch.

5. A Linguistic Model: The Tagmeme and the Syntagmeme

The descriptive language model used in this study is holistic rather than analytical. It highlights grammatical relationships within a unified construction rather than the isolated functions of the individual constituents. The use of the syntagmeme as the minimal integral unit of grammatical relationship permits a synthetic approach to syntax. It is a development from tagmemics, which it presupposes, and exploits the implicit heuristic value of both immediate constituent analysis and of transformational grammar. This is not the place to present in detail the theoretical undergirding of the model used.[1] Its utility for the complete and efficient description of a body of linguistic data may be evaluated in the results given below.

The concept of the tagmeme was developed by Kenneth L. Pike from potential in the doctrine of Leonard Bloomfield. The history of the idea is traced in Pike's paper "On tagmemes née grammemes." [2] The mature statement is Pike's *Language in relation to a unified theory of the structure of human behavior* (The Hague, 1967) .[3]

The tagmeme as a basic unit of grammatical description is defined as "the correlation of a grammatical function or slot with a class of mutually substitutable items occurring in that slot." [4] While the tagmemic model utilizes certain identification procedures found also in immediate constituent analysis, it offers more flexibility, especially in doing justice to the hierarchical features of grammatical structure and to the functional equivalence of forms on different levels of structure, thus breaking the morphology-versus-syntax deadlock. It also avoids the ambiguity impasses often met in immediate constituent analysis because of the latter's use of successive binary cuts.[5] The pedagogical value of tagmemics may be seen in the series of beginning texts inaugurated by Velma Pickett [6] and continued by Benjamin Elson[7] through the work of Elson and Pickett quoted above (n. 4) . Some idea of the productivity of tagmemic methods may be gained from Kenneth L. Pike, "A Guide to Publications Related to Tagmemic Theory" *Current Trends in Linguistics:* Vol. III: Theoretical Foundations, Thomas A. Sebeok, ed. (The Hague: Mouton, 1966) , pp. 365-94. The present writer wishes to acknowledge the stimulus obtained from two full studies of Mexican Indian languages.[8]

There has been little application of the methods of descriptive linguistics, of any school, to the Semitic languages. A pilot study by Robert E. Longacre[9] applied tagmemic theory to the description of one class of verb clauses in a small corpus of biblical Hebrew, with a rather loose use of semantic criteria for the provisional identification of class members.

The analytical techniques which tagmemics shares with immediate constituent analysis have perpetuated an emphasis on the function of isolated constituents rather than on grammatical relationships exercised mutually in constructions. Development toward a more holistic approach through the concept of the syntagmeme has been latent in the definition of the tagmeme from the beginning, since the "slot" as function can be identified only through function in relationship to the linguistic environment, or even sometimes in relationship to the nonverbal behavioral context. This need comes nearer to expression in the latest of the series of texts noted above: for example, "this relation is included in the slot," [10] a statement that warrants fuller theoretical investigation.

The typical syntagmeme is a relationship between two tagmemes whose functions are mutually self-defining within the integral construction that expounds the syntagmeme. Such syntagmemes are manifested in word-level constructions, phrase-level constructions, clause-level constructions, interclause constructions, and so on up the hierarchy, as well as in constructions that cut across levels. Put simply, the focus is on how an utterance holds together, not primarily on how it may be taken apart. The method is thus open to the insights of generative[11] and transformational [12] grammar.

The concept of the syntagmeme as a generalization of grammatical *relationship* is thus different from the term *syntagme* as used by F. de Saussure[13] to refer to a strongly unified and often idiomatic complex which may be a word, a phrase, or a clause; for him the emphasis in on its exocentric unity, not on its inner structure.[14] Following Shcherba,[15] Soviet linguists have used the term *syntagma* to describe compound words characteristic of Sanskrit, German, and other languages, or else to refer to "a rhythmically unified group of words which have a completeness of meaning." [16] Our usage differs also from the *syntagmatik* of Hjelmslev.[17] Nor is it the same in purpose as the term *syntagmeme* used for a while by Pike to replace his earlier *uttereme;*[18] he extended it to cover constructions of tagmeme sequences, that is, clause types.[19] This has real advantages, since our restriction of the syntagmeme to a minimal integral relationship treats too narrowly the functioning of tagmemes in pairs and so exposes the model to the dangers of rigidly binary analysis. This limitation can be overcome by viewing the clause also as a holistic construction, while keeping in mind the variety of relationships manifested within it.

6. Grammatical Constructions and Relationships in Verbless Clauses

The sentences of Hebrew may be represented as follows:
$$\text{Se} \; --> \; \text{Cl}_1, \text{Cl}_2, \text{Cl}_3, \ldots \; \text{Re}_1, \text{Re}_2, \text{Re}_3, \ldots$$
A sentence (Se) consists of one or more clauses (Cl) together with any items (relators [Re]) whose function it is to relate the clauses to one another in the unity of the sentence.

When a sentence is one clause, that clause is independent and may also be called a simple sentence. When a sentence contains two clauses, either (i) one is a constituent in the other; the including clause is independent, and the included clause is dependent: or (ii) neither is a constituent of the other; the clauses are interdependent, and the sentence is a construction above clause-level. And so on for sentences containing more than two clauses.

The crudeness of these statements may be excused on the grounds that sentence structure as such is not here the primary object of investigation. The inner structure of verbless clauses is the chief concern, and their functions in sentences are examined only to the extent that external function is related to internal structure. A relator which simultaneously exercises both external and internal functions within a clause, for example, a referential pronoun or a conjunction which is at the same time an adverb, will be viewed here primarily as a constituent of the clause.

In relationship to its context, each clause may then be represented as

$$\pm \text{ Re } + \text{ Cl}$$

where Re (=Relator) signals the function of the clause, and Cl (=Clause) is an exocentric construction, functioning as a single item in the larger sentence structure that environs it, while having its own inner structure within which all constituent tagmemes mutually exercise all their grammatical relationships.

$$\text{Re } --> + (\text{Ind, Co, Sub, Adn})$$

The relator may be any one of the four kinds of signals of the grammatical relationship of the clause as a whole with its environment.

Ind=Signal of independence, when the clause has no grammatical relationship with its linguistic environment.

Co=Signal of coordination, when the clause is linked in sequence with another clause.

Sub=Signal of subordination, when the clause is linked by a subordinating conjunction to a neighboring clause.

Adn=Signal of adnominal relationship, when a clause is a tagmeme in a noun phrase. In this endocentric construction a clause stands in apposition with the head noun (or noun equivalent) of the phrase.

$$\text{Ind } --> \emptyset$$

The signal of independence is the absence of a signal of any of the other three relationships.

$$\text{Co } --> + (\emptyset, \text{'}\bar{o}, \text{'}ap, gam, w^e-, k\bar{\imath})$$

The most common coordinating conjunction is w^e-, "and." [1] Zero ($\emptyset$) is a member of the set Co because a coordinated clause may lack an explicit relator. What the signal is in such a case is a problem in sentence structure. For the sake of maximum objectivity, such clauses are listed in the present study as independent.

Sub $\longrightarrow$ $+$ (*'ăšer, 'im, kī, lākēn, 'al-kēn*)

It is possible that $\emptyset$ is also Sub, but this can be established only when the subordinate function of the clause is signaled in some way, perhaps purely semantic. For the sake of objectivity such clauses will be classified as independent.

So-called conjunctions *ba'ăšer,* etc., are not included in Sub. A clause related by such a signal has the structure of a preposition phrase (Pp $+$ NEq), where NEq is a clause nominalized by *'ăšer* and so belongs to the fourth clause subset.

Adn $\longrightarrow$ $+$ ($\emptyset$, *'ăšer,* *z-, š-*)

When a clause stands in apposition with a noun (equivalent), but an explicit nominalizer is lacking, that is Adn $= \emptyset$, the function of the clause is usually not in doubt, so such clauses will be classified here as adnominal and not as independent.

Nominalized clauses may exercise other nounlike functions besides modifying a noun in apposition. The symbol Nom represents any member of this set, whatever its function, as well as its marker.

In some cases the relator may have more than one function, so the category of the clause containing it will be equivocal. For example, *kī* may coordinate or subordinate; *'ăšer* may subordinate or nominalize. Sometimes *wᵉ–* introduces circumstantial information which has a subordinate function in discourse. In this study, formal considerations are given priority, and the common function of a relator is ascribed to all its occurrences. The use of *'im* with negative or interrogative meaning is semantically related to its syntactic function as a subordinating conjunction, so this distinction will not be made in classifying it.

There are three kinds of clauses in Hebrew—verbal, quasi-verbal (p. 23), and verbless. All that follows is restricted to the last of these.

Cl $\longrightarrow$ $+$Core$/$($\pm$Mg)$_n$

Any clause consists of a core plus any number of optional margins, in various sequences. A tagmeme Mg is marginal in a structural sense, not necessarily physically, since it may be before, after, or within the core. A marginal modifier is related to the core as a whole rather than to any one tagmeme within it.

Core $\longrightarrow$ $+$S$/+$P

S$=$Subject

P$=$Predicate

The clause core consists of an obligatory subject and an obligatory predicate; it manifests the syntagmeme of predication.

The two possible sequences S–P and P–S yield the two major form sets of verbless clauses. The subject and/or the predicate may be either continuous, S or P, or discontinuous, S.... ...S or P.... ...P. The subject may be simple, S, or it may be suspended and resumed, SSus,SRes. These possibilities give rise to the numerous core patterns shown in Table 2.

When the structure of the core is complicated by the occurrence of either discontinuity or of resumption, or both, the minimum mani- festation of the $<S/P>$ relationship may be called the nucleus.

When S or P or both are discontinuous, the sequence in the nucleus is that of the head of the subject phrase and the head of the predicate phrase, all discontinuous phrases being endocentric.[2] When the subject or predicate is suspended, the sequence in the nucleus is the sequence of the resumptive pronoun and the predicate or subject.

$$Mg \; --> \; \pm Md, \; \pm Voc, \; \pm Exc$$

Md=Modifier, any indicator of manner, of spacial reference, tem- poral reference, etc., including subordinate clauses which modify the clause core as a whole.

Voc=Vocative

Exc=Exclamation

A typical verbless clause is one in which two nouns are related as S and P. Any constituent that functions as S or P may be viewed as a noun equivalent, including pronouns, adverbs, prepositional phrases, nominalized clauses, verbal nouns (participles and infinitives), as well as nouns (indefinite, definite, suffixed) and noun phrases.

A noun phrase is an endocentric construction in which two or more noun equivalents stand in one or more of the following relationships:

$<A>$ Apposition

$<C>$ Coordination

$<Ct>$ Construct

$<M>$ Modification

When S or P consists of a phrase constituted by two or more noun equivalents related in any of these ways, the category of the phrase as a whole in its tagmemic function is that of the head noun. Thus in the apposition noun phrase *'abrāhām 'ābīkā*, "Abraham your father" (Gen. 28:13) (Np $<A>$ Ns), the head is Np, and the phrase is an expanded variant of Np. In *benī 'ēśāw*, "my son Esau" (Gen. 27:24) (Ns $<A>$ Np), the head is Ns, and the phrase is an expanded variant of Ns.

It is useful to distinguish the form categories shown in Table 1 as possible subjects and predicates of verbless clauses. The items are arranged with the most definite at the top and the least definite at the bottom, in a descending scale of definiteness.

Part II

The Interpretation of the Evidence

7. The Data

All the verbless clauses in the Pentateuch are listed in the Corpus. The arrangement of the sets and subsets is explained on pages 51-52.

A schedule of occurrences of each attested core pattern is given in Tables 7-15 (pp. 112-20). From these results the data in Table 2 have been consolidated.

Obviously, absolute precision cannot be claimed for these figures. Apart from the errors inevitably present when organizing such a vast body of evidence, many of the analytical judgments on difficult texts have uncertainty in them.

The Pentateuch contains 2,044 verbless clauses. 1,857 are declarative (Table 2); 78 are precative (Table 14); 109 are interrogative (Table 15). Prescriptive clauses are not distinguished from declarative. They are found chiefly in the specifications for the tabernacle. The clauses in ##43 and 44 are typical. Comparison of #52 <Ns–Num> and #122 <Num–Ns> shows that both sequences of S and P are used with the same items.

Table 2 summarizes the occurrences of the eight major kinds of declarative clause. Each type is well represented except nominalized clauses with sequence P–S, of which there are only 33 examples (Table 13). The fact that about one-third of declarative clauses (606 out of 1,857) have the sequence P–S is enough to suggest that this important pattern cannot be explained simply as an exception to the S–P pattern.

Thirty-seven percent of independent declarative verbless clauses (261 out of 718) have sequence P–S. Sixty-two percent of subordinate declarative verbless clauses have sequence P–S (202 out of 325). But only nineteen percent of coordinate declarative verbless clauses (110 out of 572) have sequence P–S. This shows at once that the preferred sequence varies with the external function of the clause.

8. Clauses of Identification and Classification

In order to find correlation patterns, that is, in order to have an empirical basis for the statement of cooccurrence rules or laws of distri-

31

bution, it is essential to vary only two parameters at a time. There are 359 independent declarative verbless clauses which have a pronoun for subject. They differ only in (i) the category of the predicate, and (ii) the sequence of the nucleus. Correlation between these two variables is shown in Table 3. In compiling this table from data in Tables 7 and 8, clauses with discontinuity or with resumption in S or P and clauses with marginal modifiers have all been excluded so as to restrict the variables absolutely to two only.

Table 3 shows that there is a correspondence between nuclear sequence and the placement of the predicate on the descending scale of definiteness in Table 1. This is seen in the skewness of the figures, bunched to the top of the S–P column and to the bottom of the P–S column.

Generalizations emerge when three main degrees of definiteness are distinguished. (i) When the predicate is definite (items 1-8 in Table 1), the preferred sequence is S–P (223 out of 231). (ii) When the predicate is indefinite (items 12-18 in Table 1), the preferred sequence is P–S (75 out of 86). (iii) When the predicate is Ns or an expansion of Ns (items 9 and 10 in Table 1), the occurrences of both sequences are of the same order—S–P thirteen times, P–S nineteen times.

These patterns are so consistent that they may be made the basis of grammatical rules or of the recognition of two kinds of predication.

When both S and P are definite, the predicate has total semantic overlap with the subject; that is, each has exactly the same referent. The predicate supplies the identity of the subject. This may be called a clause of *identification*. The nuclear sequence is S–P.

When S is definite and P is indefinite (in the typical and commonest case P is an indefinite noun, Ni), the predicate has partial semantic overlap with the subject; that is, it refers to the general class of which the subject is a member. The predicate states the class of the subject. This may be called a clause of *classification*. The nuclear sequence is P–S.

#1 contains typical clauses of identification; #94 contains typical clauses of classification.

When P is Ns or one of its expansions, a semantic analysis of each case shows that such a predicate may serve either to identify or to classify the subject. This depends in part on the referent, in part on the intention of the speaker to highlight either the identity or the character of the subject. The proper sequence may be chosen for one or other of these effects. Table 3 shows that each sequence occurs fairly frequently.

The apparent equivocation in the behavior of Ns as P with definite S may be explained in terms of the intermediate definiteness of a suffixed noun. An indefinite noun like *bēn*, "[a] son," refers to any member of a general class. The definite *habbēn*, "the son," refers to a specific individual. The form of the suffixed noun *b^enō*, "his son," does not indicate whether the noun is definite or indefinite; that depends on what it refers to. If a man has several sons, *b^enō* may refer to any one of them but does not establish the identity of any one of them; *b^enō* is then indefinite, although not as indefinite as *bēn*. If a man has only one son, *b^enō* refers to that individual and so is definite. We conclude that a suffixed noun may either identify the subject in sequence Pr–Ns or classify the subject in sequence Ns–Pr. See further discussion on pages 46-47.

These results are supported by three transformations. (i) When transforming a predicate into an attribute ("the man is good" --> "the good man") identifying predicates become definite attributes, classifying predicates become indefinite attributes. Ns may have either kind of attribute: compare Gen. 43:29 ("your youngest brother") with Deut. 21:20 ("a stubborn and rebellious son of ours"). (ii) When modifying a predicate with a prepositional phrase, identifying predicates use the nominalizer as a mark of definiteness (*hā'ănāšim 'ăšer 'ittō*, "the men with him" [Gen. 24:32]); classifying predicates have the indefinite prepositional phrase alone (*māqōm lagg^emallīm*, "a place for the camels" [Gen. 24:31]). Ns may have either kind of modifier: a phrase like *bētō 'aḥărāw*, "his family after him" (Gen. 18:19), shows that it may be indefinite. This matches the contrast between the restrictive and nonrestrictive use of a relative clause in English; but the formal ambiguity of the latter, which can be resolved only by the use of intonation or punctuation, does not exist in Hebrew. (iii) When transforming the predicate of a verbless clause into the object of a verb, identifying predicates correspond to objects with *nota accusativi 'et*, a correlate of definiteness; classifying predicates become objects with no *nota accusativi*, as befits their indefiniteness. Ns may or may not use *'et*, depending on its referent.

So far the results have been based exclusively on verbless declarative clauses in which the subject is a pronoun, without margins, discontinuity, or resumption. Table 4 shows the incidence of all kinds of clauses in which the subject is definite (items 1–8 of Table 1), including those with margins, discontinuity, or resumption.

Table 4 confirms the results already obtained. Clauses of identification (S and P both definite) have sequence S–P in the overwhelming number of cases (436 out of 462). Clauses of classification prefer the sequence P–S (286 out of 384). Clauses with P=Ns or N <Ct> Ns occur with either sequence: 43 with S–P, 41 with P–S.

Clauses in which P=Numi prefer the sequence S–P. Clauses in which the predicate is a prepositional phrase are fairly evenly divided between the two sequences.

9. Clauses with a Participle as Predicate

Table 4 shows that there are 332 clauses in which a definite subject has a participle or a participle phrase as predicate. The sequence S–P is used 304 times, so this is clearly the normal pattern. It may be noted that the biggest contribution to this total comes from nominalized clauses; furthermore, nominalized clauses with participles are the biggest group of nominalized clauses, and of these the majority come from Deuteronomy. But the pattern is normal for all sources.

From the formal point of view, a participle is like an indefinite noun. As *nomen agentis* it is readily used as *nomen professionis*. *Meraggelim 'attem*, "you are spies" (Gen. 42:9), has been placed in #94, not classified as <Pti–Pr>. This formal similarity makes the grammatical contrast between the two parts of speech all the more striking. Clauses with participles, with normal sequence S–P, are a category distinct from clauses of classification, with normal sequence P–S. As such they may be called *verbal*.

The contrast between sequence P–S when P is Ni and S–P when P is Pti is exhibited in Jos. 9:16: *wayyišme'ū kī qerōbīm hēm 'ēlāyw ūbeqirbō hēm yōšebīm*. The effect is chiastic, but both clauses are normal.

10. The Effect of Margins on Structure

Clauses with optional marginal modifiers have been listed separately in the Corpus. They may be found by means of the general Contents.

Margins may be placed before, after, or within the clause nucleus. Exclamations, vocatives, and modals (including negators) commonly precede the nucleus; adverbs and prepositional phrases may be added at any point.

There is no indication that the addition of a marginal modifier causes any perturbation in the normal structure of a clause. A few apparent exceptions are found, of course. For example, the sequence S–P is abnormal in ##66, 67, 355, for these are clauses of classification. But each of these clauses has its own difficulty; they do not change the overall picture.

11. Sequence in Coordinated Clauses

The figures in Table 2 show that the sequence S–P is relatively more frequent in coordinated clauses than in other types. The number of P–S clauses is only about nineteen percent of the total. The reason for this may be seen from Table 4. Clauses of classification are rarely met nominalized—only seven examples—so little can be said about the patterns here. Subordinate clauses include many clauses of classification; there are 118 in which P is Ni or N <Ct> Ni, and of these, 115 have sequence P–S. This confirms the conclusion already reached, that P–S is normal when P is indefinite.

But this rule is *not* followed in coordinate clauses. Here even clauses of classification prefer the sequence S–P, which is found in 57 cases out of 80. This striking inversion may be correlated with a special function that such clauses have in discourse. A detailed study of the linguistic environment of the clauses in ##187 and 191, which are prime examples, shows that they are typically *circumstantial* in function.

On the other hand, not one of the coordinated clauses with sequence P–S is circumstantial. The simple construction w– + <Ni–S> is found only twice (##282, 287—the latter doubtful). All the other examples (##283, 301, 302, 306, 309, 312, 313, 316, 319) contain various signals that the clauses are independent or linked only loosely with the preceding context.

There is a third sequence pattern with coordinate clauses: two or more clauses of identical structure are joined by w–. #175 contains examples.

When the predicate is indefinite, inversion of the normal sequence from P–S to S–P is a signal along with the use of w– that the clause is circumstantial. The strictness with which Hebrew verbless clauses follow these patterns suggests that some of the asyndetic clauses of classification with the abnormal sequence S–P are in fact circumstantial in function. In such cases the inversion of the normal sequence is in itself the signal of this circumstantial function. (See page 43 for more on this.)

Coordinated clauses of identification (both S and P definite) have the sequence S–P 115 out of 119 times (Table 4). Only the context shows whether they are independent (adjoined), linked in sequence (conjoined), or circumstantial (subjoined).

12. Discontinuity and Resumption

So far the discussion has focused on the minimal nucleus of the clause, whether S–P or P–S. In 331 clauses the core is more complex due to various patterns of discontinuity and of pleonasm.

There are thirteen core patterns in verbless clauses in the Pentateuch. These are listed in Table 2, together with the number of clauses which have each core pattern. 142 have nucleus S–P; 189 have nucleus P–S, with discontinuity.

Discontinuity in the subject occurs 71 times—only once with nucleus P–S (#439). The core S...–P ...S, which occurs in independent (29 times), coordinate (39 times), and subordinate (twice) clauses, is characteristic of the lists of names and other statistics common in the priestly material. See ##74-79; 255-263. The two non-contiguous parts of the subject stand in the grammatical relationship of apposition, the head being an introductory pronoun. The first part, S...–P, serves as a title for the following data, ...S. Compare #18 and Gen. 17:10; 20:13.

Patterns of discontinuity in S other than in an apposition phrase are less common. The discontinuity in Gen. 24:25 (#80) breaks up a coordination phrase. The meaning of Gen. 2:9 (#267) is clarified when a similar construction is recognized here.

The core P... S–...P occurs 39 times (##81-83; 271-273; 357-359). In every case the head of the predicate is a participle, which stands in the normal verbal sequence with the subject. See p. 48.

The *casus pendens* is a more familiar construction. The core SSus, SRes–P occurs 29 times. The resumptive (pleonastic) pronoun is considered to be the nuclear subject in our analysis (see p. 23). Albrecht (pp. 249-253) discusses the role of the pleonastic pronoun as a virtual copula. In 'ānōkī 'ānōkī yahwe, "I, I am Yahweh" (Isa. 43:11; compare Isa. 43:25; 51:12; and Deut. 32:39 in #360) the suspended pronoun is resumed by itself and is hardly a copula. In Ezek. 22:24, however, a second person pronoun is resumed by a third person pronoun, which could be called a copula: 'atte 'ereṣ lō' meṭōhārā hī', "you are a land not cleaned."

We have not identified the second pronoun in a sentence like 'ēlle hēm benē yišmā''ēl (#5) as resumptive or copula, but as a duplication; that is, 'ēlle hēm is a compound pronoun like ma-zzō't.

Resumption of a preposed predicate with nucleus S–P is not common—three times (#89), all curious clauses. Discontinuity and resumption can occur in the same clause (#280).

The bottom half of Table 2 shows that a disproportionate number of clauses with discontinuity in the predicate occur when the nucleus is P–S. In fact, over thirty percent of P–S clauses have a discontinuous predicate or resumption. The high incidence of discontinuous predicates (153 examples) is even more impressive when further facts are noticed. These are set out in Table 5.

In most of the 417 clauses with simple core P–S, the predicate is simple and indivisible, generally a single word. Here the possibility of discontinuity does not arise at all. Nor is discontinuity likely when the predicate is a construct phrase, although it is possible, as Gen. 49:3 shows (#160). A predicate consisting of a noun (or "adjective") negated by lō' is never divided; and a numeral phrase is never broken up, unless in Gen. 42:13.

When the predicate is a participle phrase, or a noun phrase with apposition, coordination, or modification by an adverb or by a prepositional phrase, discontinuity is not only possible, it occurs in the majority of cases. Table 5 shows that there are 185 clauses with a predicate of the kind in which discontinuity might occur; and of these, 153 have a predicate divided asunder by the subject. The proportion of continuous to discontinuous phrases as predicate is about equal for apposition and coordination, but in all other constructions, especially modification of a noun by a prepositional phrase, discontinuity is the general rule.

The same kind of discontinuity is shown in precative (##493-495; 499-501) and interrogative (##532; 549-551) clauses.

The contrasting positions of the resumptive pronoun in <SSus, PrRes–P>, when P is definite, and in <SSus,P–PrRes>, when P is indefinite, confirm results already established for clauses with simple cores. The former are clauses of identification; the latter are clauses of classification; and the placement of the resumptive pronoun secures the right sequence in the nucleus. See Rules 2 (p. 42) and 4 (p. 45).

13. Clauses with Indefinite Subjects

The 1,450 clauses studied in Table 4 all have definite subjects. In the remaining declarative clauses the subject is Ns or some other member of items 9-18 in Table 1.

There are 244 clauses in which the subject is Ns, N <Ct> Ns, or the like. These exhibit the same patterns as were found in Table 4, suggesting that Ns is definite when it is subject. The sequence S–P is preferred when P is definite—identification (for example, #47); and when P is Pti—verbal (for example, #49). When P is Ni or N <Ct>

37

Ni, P–S is preferred in independent and in subordinate clauses; but S–P predominates in coordinate clauses, since most of them are circumstantial.

There are 101 clauses with Ns as S and Num as P, most of which specify dimensions or statistics and are assigned to the priestly source for this reason. The sequence S–P is preferred for counting (for example, #52) ; the sequence P–S is preferred for dimensions of length, breadth, and height (for example, #122). The same kinds of clauses are frequently linked in coordination without inversion. (See #226 for S–P, #290 for P–S.)

The remaining 163 declarative verbless clauses have an indefinite subject—items 11-18 in Table 1. The predicate is usually indefinite also. In more than half, P is a prepositional phrase, and both sequences are well represented.

For other combinations the number of examples is not large enough to admit of significant generalizations. Some interesting individual cases will be discussed in detail below.

14. Precative Clauses

Wishes are commonly expressed in verbless clauses in which the predicate is a participle or a prepositional phrase. Such clauses are found in ##474-501; the statistics are gathered together in Table 14. Both sequences S–P and P–S are met. Their distribution is shown in Table 6. This shows that the sequence P–S is preferred when the predicate is a participle; this is the inverse of the declarative sequence.[1] The sequence S–P predominates in precative clauses in which the predicate is a prepositional phrase. This also is the reverse of a common declarative sequence, although here the picture is less clear-cut. This problem is discussed in more detail below, pages 49-50.

15. Interrogative Clauses

The 109 interrogative verbless clauses in the Pentateuch are given in ##502-555. A schedule of occurrences is given in Table 15.

The three kinds of interrogation are discussed on page 24. In a request for identification or classification, $m\bar{\imath}$ or $ma-$ functions as predicate (see p. 21). Clauses containing these interrogators are listed separately (##502-519). There are 64 such clauses, and the sequence is <Int–S> in 62 of them.

Another item rarely precedes the interrogator. In Num. 16:11 (#519) the preposed item is a suspended subject, resumed later.

Other possible, though less clear examples are Gen. 23:15, 31:32; Num. 13:18. The normal core sequence <Int–S> is present in each instance, even if the subject is a pleonastic pronoun.

This fact throws into relief the two clauses in which the sequence <S–Int> seems to occur (#515). According to Albrecht (p. 223), these are the only examples of this sequence in the Old Testament. The clause in Exod. 16:7—*wᵉnaḥnū mā kī tallī(w)nū ʿālēnū,* "and we are what that you murmur against us?"—may be compared with Num. 16:11—*wᵉʾahărōn ma-hūʾ kī tallī(w)nū ʿālāyw,* "and Aaron, what is he that you murmur against him?" This suggests that Exod. 16:7 and 8 are not authentic realizations of the sequence <S–Int>. Rather are they elliptical for **wᵉnaḥnū mā <naḥnū>* . . . , "and we, what are we . . . ?" The first pronoun is not the subject, but *casus pendens;* the resumptive pronoun, present in Num. 16:11, and which gives the normal sequence <Int–Pr> in the core, is lacking in Exod. 16:7 and 8. Compare: *mī ʾānōkī kī ʾēlēk ʾel-parʿō,* "who am I, that I should go to Pharaoh?" (Exod. 3:11).

Other interrogators similarly come first in the clause (except for conjunctions). In such clauses S and P are in the sequence that they normally have in declarative clauses. Thus *hăze ʾăḥīkem* . . . , "Is this your brother . . . ?" (Gen. 43:29; #521), has sequence S–P normal for a clause of identification. *Haʿeprātī ʾattā,* "are you an Ephrathite?" (Judg. 12:5), has sequence P–S normal for a clause of classification. In other words, the interrogator introduces no perturbation into clause structure and can be viewed as querying the statement as a whole.[1] Gen. 4:9 (#535) seems to violate the rule that a participle as predicate follows the subject, but here *šōmēr* is not really a verb ("watching"), although it has an object, but a noun, and could be classed as Ni.

Coordinated interrogative clauses are coordinated only with other interrogative clauses (#515-518), or else the conjunction introduces a suspended item (##519, 553, 554). But see #555.

16. Rules and Exceptions

The outlines of the grammar of the verbless clause in Hebrew are now clear. This makes it possible to examine more carefully the clauses which seem to break the rules.

Rule 1: The sequence is S–P in a clause of identification, in which both S and P are definite.

The subject of such a clause is most commonly a pronoun; compare Table 3 with Table 4. Identification clauses in ##1-22 in which S= Pr have three main functions in discourse.

(i) They identify a person by name, either in answer to a question (Gen. 27:19; but compare Gen. 24:24), or more often as the self-identification of a speaker at the beginning (sometimes at the end) of a pronouncement. The inclusion of Exod. 20:5 (=Deut. 5:9) in #323 is a departure from the traditional: "I, Yahweh your god, am a jealous god. . . ." The reasons for this are: (a) The clauses in ##1 and 323 suggest a similar self-announcement here (compare Exod. 20:2). (b) The indefinite predicate '*ēl qannā*' requires sequence P–S by Rule 3. Similar arguments apply to Num. 14:14; 35:34. The statement '*ēliyyā hattišbī hū*', "he is Elijah the Tishbite" (II Kings 1:8) is a striking exception (compare I Sam. 28:14). Here, for once, the idea of emphasis may be appropriate.

(ii) The pronouns *hū*', *hī*', *hēmmā* are used as subjects of clauses which answer questions (for example, Gen. 24:65) or which serve as glosses (for example, Gen. 14:7). They refer back to something already mentioned. Only in Deut. 34:4 (#12) does *zō't* function in this way. All other clauses in #12 are P, not D.

(iii) The pronouns *ze*, *zō't*, '*elle* occur characteristically in clauses which serve as titles, occasionally as colophons. This is clearly their function in ##74-79. They refer forward to something not yet mentioned. Only in Gen. 41:28 (#12) does *hū*' have this introductory function, and even here it could point backwards. A comparison of Gen. 2:23 (#67) with Exod. 22:26 (#20) highlights the peculiar use of *zō't* in the former; we would expect *hī*'. The same expectation throws doubt on the traditional interpretation of *ze 'ēlī*, "this is my god" (Exod. 15:2; #19), which could even be '*ēlī ze* by Rule 6 (compare Isa. 44:17; Ps. 22:11; 63:2; 118:28; 140:7). Instead of normalizing the sequence or changing *ze* to *hū*', perhaps *z–* (**zu*) is determinative. Recognition of postpositive conjunctions leads to the translation:

> And I shall praise him who is my God,
> And I shall exalt him who is my father's God.

Even though both subject and predicate in an identifying clause are definite, the predicate is generally less definite than the subject. In some languages even proper nouns can, on occasion, function as count nouns,[1] and so be less than absolutely definite. Biblical Hebrew does not present examples of modification of a proper noun by quantifiers; but the noun categories in Table 1 may still be viewed as standing in decreasing order of definiteness. Otherwise it would not be possible to speak about sequence in clauses of identification: if both S and P were identical in definiteness, it would not be possible to say which was which.

Viewed in this light, $k\bar{o}l$, "all," is seen to be a special kind of noun; phrases containing it seem to be always definite and nearly always come first in the clause. #6 shows it to be a kind of numeral. Perhaps it could be called a pronoun; compare Exod. 12:33 (#23). Clauses with $k\bar{o}l$ in S have sequence S–P, even when Rule 3 is violated, as in Gen. 31:12; Exod. 38:16; Isa. 56:10; Jer. 5:16; Ezek. 32:22, 23, 24, 25, 26; Nah. 3:1; Mal. 2:17; Ezra 6:20. S–P remains even when $k\bar{o}l$ is used in resumption, and Rule 4 might be expected to operate (#366). Only in Deut. 4:4 (#316) and in Deut. 29:22 (#120) does $k\bar{o}l$ fail to come first, and this is a difficult clause in any case. But in ##162 (compare 171), 165, 172, 173, $k\bar{o}l$ stands in *casus pendens*, and the normal sequence of Rule 4 is secured by resumption.

It has been suggested above that the predicate is usually less definite semantically than the subject, even when both are formally definite. Since Table 1 lists N <Ct> Np as less definite than Np, a clause like $\check{s}\bar{e}m$ '$\bar{e}\check{s}et$-'$abr\bar{a}m$ $\check{s}\bar{a}ray$, "Abram's wife's name is Sarai" (Gen. 11:29; #35), has an unexpected sequence. Some of the other examples in #35 may not be well-formed clauses at all, but rather distributive items in lists. The sequence in Gen. 11:29 proves to be normal; clauses in which S contains $\check{s}\bar{e}m$ have sequence S–P in nearly every case, as if $\check{s}\bar{e}m$ in itself is definite. There are thirty-nine examples in ##35, 42, 47, 200, 214, 220, 229, 452. The name itself is the information supplied, and Rule 6 does not operate. The same is true of the fifteen clauses in ##232, 236, which Albrecht (p. 254) analyzed as P–S. This is wrong. They identify the leader (S–P); they do not state the rank of the person named (P–S), as in Rule 3. Compare Neh. 11:14, 22, and Judg. 4:2, where the equivalence of $\check{s}ar$ with 'al in Num. 10 (#285) suggests that here too 'al is a title and not a preposition, a fact already well known from other connections.

The reverse sequence, that is, with $\check{s}\bar{e}m$ in S following P occurs only three times in the Pentateuch. In Exod. 15:3 (##28, 119) $yahwe$ $\check{s}^em\bar{o}$ is a resumptive phrase with a special liturgical function; compare Amos 4:13; 5:8, 27; 9:6, and often in Isaiah and Jeremiah. In Gen. 17:15 (#390) the inverted sequence secures contrastive focus on the name itself—"*but* her name is Sarah"; compare I Sam. 25:25. Sequence P–S is used also in Gen. 28:19 (#303; compare Judg. 18:29, contrast Jos. 15:15; Isa. 5:7). See Albrecht's comments (pp. 220, 254). The unusual sequence P–S in $qann\bar{a}$' $\check{s}^em\bar{o}$—unusual because $Qann\bar{a}$' is surely a name and not an indefinite noun in Exod. 34:14 (#465) —

is not, as so often in other connections, a signal of a circumstantial function, but of a relative clause; compare II Sam. 20:21; I Kings 13:2; Job 1:1. It is the sequence S–P that is used circumstantially (##200, 214, 220, 229).

Rule 1 seems to be violated in ##90, 141, 162, 369, 408, 432, which have definite predicates N <Ct> Np, and in ##91, 169, 370, which have definite predicates N <Ct> Nd coming before the subject. The same sequence in ##310, 311, 318 is not a problem, because these clauses are circumstantial and follow Rule 5. It is noteworthy that the predicates in these apparently abnormal clauses are construct phrases. As such they are generic rather than specific and so are not absolutely definite. They follow the normal sequence for clauses of classification (Rule 3). The sequence as such makes them clauses of classification. For example, Joseph discloses himself in a clause of identification: *'ănī yōsēp* (Gen. 45:3). Rebekah replies: *bat–bᵉtū'ēl 'ānōkī* (Gen. 24:24). This classifies her as (the) daughter of Bethuel. If she had used the reverse sequence, this would have implied that her name was Bath-bethuel.

The clause *yᵉhūdā 'attā,* "you are Judah" (Gen. 49:8), violates Rule 1 and cannot be explained away as a classification clause. It is the only clause in the Pentateuch in which Np as P is abnormal. Stylistic analysis shows that translations which solve the problem by ignoring *'attā* completely, such as RSV, have missed the point. *Yᵉhūdā* is to be detached as the title of the oracle, not as vocative. The following clause is then seen to be <Pr–Nom> (#18), with nominalizer zero (compare KJV): "you (are) [the one whom] your brothers praise."

The clause *yahwe haṣṣaddīq* (Exod. 9:27) is not an illustration of Rule 1: it is not a statement of Yahweh's identity; it classifies him as the righteous one (#109).

Rule 2: A pleonastic pronoun in a clause of identification comes before the predicate, in keeping with Rule 1. Contrast Rule 4.

The pronoun *hū'* is used characteristically to refer back to the suspended subject (##84-87). By contrast, the apparently pleonastic *'ēlle* points forward to a following subject (##74-79). In other words, the cores SSus,SRes–P, and S...–P...S are distinct categories, not allo-syntagmas or free variants, and the latter does not violate Rule 2.

Rule 3: The sequence is P–S in a clause of classification, in which P is indefinite relative to S.

Apparent exceptions to this rule are met when clauses are circumstantial (Rule 5).

So long as the grammar of the nominal sentence in Hebrew was dominated by the doctrine that S–P is the normal sequence for all kinds of predication, the significance of this clause class could not be appreciated. Nearly all of the abundant examples of P–S given by Albrecht as exceptions to his S–P rule for a noun predicate (pp. 254-256) or for an adjective predicate (pp. 257-258) are pure manifestations of Rule 3 or of Rule 6. On the other hand, most of his examples for his S–P rule when P is an adjective are coordinated clauses, circumstantial in function, and so normal manifestations of Rule 5. Albrecht listed *ṭōb deḇar-yahwe 'ăšer dibbartā* (II Kings 20:19) as an exception which he explained by the length of the subject (p. 220). But the clause is normal; compare #112.

Suspicion is aroused when the sequence P–S is not realized in a clause of classification.

(i) Rule 3 is not followed when S contains *kōl* (see p. 41). Examples are found in ##25 and 26.

(ii) The predicate may be a participle, following Rule 7. For this reason *kullānū mētīm* (Exod. 12:33), which also comes under (i) immediately above, is placed in #23. Perhaps this should have been done with Num. 9:7 (#25) as well. For the same reason *'ēd* has been classified as a participle rather than as a noun in Gen. 31:50 (#29) and Gen. 31:48 (#39). The syntax of Gen. 15:1 (#25) is against identifying *māgēn*, "shield," as an indefinite noun. Better is a participle *(me)maggēn*, "benefactor," a suitable parallel to the following *śkr* (compare Gen. 14:20); or a title—*Māgān*, "Suzerain," here a divine name, following Rule 1.[2] Compare ##1, 3. In Deut. 3:5 (#25) it is better to identify *beṣūrōt* rather than *'ārīm* as P, preferring KJV to RSV, so that *kol-'ēlle 'ārīm* is S. This supports the identification of *kullām 'ănāšīm*, "all the men," with enclitic *mem*, as S in Num. 13:3 (#162). Compare ##165, 171.

(iii) Some apparent exceptions to Rule 3 are circumstantial, with S–P sequence normal for Rule 5. When *w-* is lacking, such clauses may be called parenthetical. All the clauses in ##43, 44, 46, 50 are of this kind. The sequence as such, by contrasting with Rule 3, is the signal of the circumstantial function of the clause. This accounts for the sequence in Exod. 25:36; 37:22 (#26), and in Gen. 11:10 (#32).[3] Rule 3 is against the traditional translation of *nōḥ 'īš ṣaddīq* (Gen. 6:9; #31) as a classifying clause. It could be a phrase ("Noah, a righteous man . . ."); or circumstantial ("Noah being a righteous man . . ."). Job 12:4 suggests that *ṣaddīq tāmīm* is a single phrase; compare *ṣaddīq 'attīq, ṣaddīq kabbīr*.

(iv) A construction that does not follow Rule 3 may not be a clause at all. Gen. 49:5 (#30) is an example.[4] The oracles for Gad, Asher, Naphtali, and Benjamin in Gen. 49 all begin with the tribe name as title. Compare the style of Deut. 33. "Simeon and Levi" is a similar heading. This clears up Gen. 49:21, 27 (#31), leading to translations:

> Naphtali: A hind is released;
> Sheep of the fold[5] are sold.
> Benjamin: A wolf ravens . . .

Similarly Gen. 49:14 (#33) becomes:

> Issachar: Ass-driver became resident;
> Tinker settled down.[6]

Num. 14:18 (#33) is probably not a clause but a string of epithets used in invocation or as a creed—a recognized *Gattung*. The same may be true of *yahwe 'īš milḥāmā* in Exod. 15:3 (#32) which breaks Rule 3 if it is a clause meaning "Yahweh is a man of war" (there is no problem in II Sam. 17:8, where the clause is circumstantial). Either there is apposition—"Yahweh, the one of battles," with determinative *'š*—or this is an isogloss of the title *yahwe ṣebā'ōt* (*yahwe* being verbal) meaning "he who causes the men [collective] of battle to come into existence."[7] This conclusion is supported by stylistic analysis of the sequel *yahwe šemō* (p. 41). Compare Num. 14:18.

A similar result has already been reached with Deut. 33:23 (#32), where interpreters have preferred to recognize the entire phrase as vocative—"O Naphtali, satiated with favor!" The same arguments show that Hosea 6:8 is vocative. It would break Rule 3 if it were a clause as RSV assumes.

(v) The sequence S–P, when P–S is expected, could be a signal that the clause is precative. This may account for the contrast between *dān gūr 'aryē,* "let Dan be a lioncub!" (Deut. 33:22; #32) and *gūr 'aryē yehūdā,* "Judah is a lioncub" (Gen. 49:9; #107). It could apply also to Deut. 33:23 (#32). See (iv) above.

(vi) There remains a very small number of real exceptions to Rule 3 in which the sequence S–P for a clause of classification is inexplicable. They are: Gen. 42:13; Exod. 33:5; Num. 28:14 (#26); Gen. 18:20 (#36) (which is archaic poetry; compare Gen. 1:4 [#40] and Gen. 49:15 [#56]); Gen. 2:23 (#67); Gen. 6:3 (#66). The last two are both old and difficult passages. A solution for Gen. 6:3 may lie in the use of *bśr* as at Alalakh to report malfeasance of a vassal. Ezek. 27:3 contains an exception to Rule 3.

Rule 3 makes it clear that *'ĕlōhīm* is generic in Judg. 6:31 and I Kings 18:27. It also settles the syntax of II Sam. 17:10, where *'ăšer 'ittō,* "the ones with him," is S and *benē-ḥayil* is P.

The rule P–S for verbless clauses of classification is likely to prove important in the study of comparative Semitic syntax. See ##92, 93. It supports the arguments of Giorgio Buccellati that the Akkadian stative is a nominal sentence with the same structure.[8] It is in line with P–S characteristic of personal names in Amorite which are in fact nominal sentences. These should not be considered "contrary to normal Semitic word order" as Herbert B. Huffmon suggests.[9]

Rule 4: A pleonastic pronoun in a clause of classification comes after the predicate, in keeping with Rule 3. Contrast Rule 2.

Examples are found in ##162-174; 310-320; 432-437. The contrasting patterns of Rules 2 and 4 are followed with remarkable consistency. Lev. 23:27 (#169) is an apparent exception, to be explained in terms of the discussion on pages 40-41. The same applies to ##310, 311, 432. It may be noted that Albrecht (p. 223) classifies Exod. 16:36 as S–P.

W. von Soden[10] notes that this construction appears very late in Accadian; Aramaic influence may be suspected. By the same token, West Semitic influence may be detected in this clause from Alalakh: *ᵐḪa-am-mu-ra-pi be-el URU.KI-ia ù É-ia šu-ú ù ÌR-du ša Ia-ri-im-li-im be-lì-ia šu-ú,* "Hammurapi, owner of my city and of my house (is) he, and servant of my lord Yarimlim (is) he." [11]

Rule 5: Circumstantial clauses of classification have sequence S–P, in contrast with Rules 3 and 4.

Num. 5:28 is unique in this regard (#282). When the normal sequence P–S is used in a coordinated clause of classification, it is probably not circumstantial. It may be independent; for example, *we'ĕmet haddābār* (Dan. 10:1). The independent function of the clause is usually marked by the use of *wᵉgam* or *wᵉ'ūlām* rather than *wᵉ–;* for example, Num. 13:27 (#283), Gen. 20:12 (#300), Num. 14:21 (#301), Gen. 28:19 (#303).

The noncircumstantial sequence of Rule 3 is used in a coordinated clause when it is conjoined with a clause of identical structure. Examples are found in Gen. 3:6; 49:12; Deut. 30:11. In II Sam. 17:8 the first clause follows Rule 3, the second is conjoined with it and also follows Rule 3; the third clause, however, is circumstantial and follows Rule 5. See also I Kings 3:22, which Albrecht describes as S–P (p. 257), wrongly, I think.

Numerous subordinate clauses follow Rule 3 (##374-376; 379-382; 385-387). In #333 Gen. 48:14 has been analyzed as S–P (Rule 1).

This may be correct; see #324. But it is relationship or status, not identity, that is in mind; and one might have expected *kī habbᵉkōr mᵉnašše, "for Manasseh is the firstborn" by Rule 3. Compare #369. If so, the reverse sequence actually used is a signal that the clause is circumstantial; kī must be translated "although" [12] not "for" (RSV). This is the case in Gen. 8:21 (#355).

Rule 6: When a suffixed noun is predicate, the sequence S–P (Rule 1) is used for a clause of identification in which the suffixed noun is definite; the sequence P–S (Rule 3) is used for a clause of classification in which the suffixed noun is indefinite.

See the preliminary discussion on pages 32-33. In ##19-22, 64, 86, statements of identity are secured by sequence S–P. Gen. 31:43 (#38) seems to be the only classifying clause with Ns as P using sequence S–P; contrast I Kings 3:22. The clauses in ##92, 93, 104, 371, 372, are clear examples of the use of P–S with Ns as P to assert the relationship of P to S rather than the identity of S and P.

There is redundancy in the operation of Rule 1 and of Rule 3 which is not available in the operation of Rule 6, owing to the ambiguity in Ns. When the distinction between definiteness and indefiniteness is secured either by formal (for instance, the article) or semantic (for instance, all personal names are definite) means in the predicate, such a signal operates side by side with sequence to make the clause category doubly certain. So sequence as such suggests the definiteness or indefiniteness of the predicate, irrespective of its form. When P is Ns or the like, it is clause sequence alone that indicates whether it is definite or indefinite. The sequence S–P identifies S as P, and suggests that Ns is definite; the sequence P–S classifies S as P and suggests that Ns is indefinite in relation to S. It is even possible for sequence P–S to suggest that nouns more definite than Ns, for example N <Ct> Np or N <Ct> Nd, are indefinite in relation to S. (See discussion on p. 42.)

In answer to the question, "Who is that man?" hū' 'ădōnī, "he is my master" (Gen. 24:65) identifies Isaac. The slave had only one master; 'ădōnī is unique and definite. The same effect is seen in a clause like 'ănī binkā bᵉkōrᵉkā 'ēśāw, "I am your son, your firstborn, Esau" (Gen. 27:32). Isaac had two sons; so binkā alone would refer to any member of that class of persons. But here binkā, or rather the phrase of which it is the head, is seen to be definite, both by its placement and also by the nouns in apposition with it, especially the proper name 'ēśāw.

On the other hand, in *'āḥī hū'*, "he is my brother" (Gen. 20:5), the position of the predicate shows that it is indefinite. The clause does not assert Abraham's identity, but his relationship to Sarah. It classifies him. As so used, *'āḥī* is generic and indefinite; but it does not necessarily imply that Sarah had other brothers.

There are a few clauses with structure <Np–Ns> in which it is better to identify the proper noun as the predicate. Exod. 15:3 (#119) has already been discussed (p. 41). It has also been proposed that the personal name is predicate in Exod. 9:27 (#109). A comparison of versions shows how problematical the grammar of Exod. 4:14 (#529) is. It is possible that it states that Moses' brother (S) is Aaron the Levite (P), P being discontinuous. Another clause of celebrated difficulty is Deut. 6:4—*yahwe 'ĕlōhēnū yahwe 'eḥād*. The many proposed translations face objections of various kinds. "The LORD our God is one LORD" (RSV) analyzes < (Np <A> Ns) – (Np <A> Num) >, and implies that Np can be a count noun. This is avoided in "The LORD our God, the LORD is one" (RSVMg), which analyzes < (Np <A> Ns) Sus,NpRes–Num>. But both these interpretations collide with Rule 3, extended to numerals, as clauses in # #150, 157 suggest; resumptive *hū'* at the end would be more natural (Rule 4). "The LORD is our God, the LORD is one" (RSVMg) makes two distinct clauses, in each of which Yahweh is S. Objections to the second of these have already been given. But the first is not satisfactory either; for the concern is not the identity of Yahweh. Finally "The LORD is our God, the LORD alone" (RSVMg, JPS), besides the objection already given to the first clause, involves a strange use of *'eḥād* with the meaning of *lebaddō*. A combination of Rule 3 and Rule 6 points to another solution. The confession goes with the first commandment, "You shall not have other gods besides me" (Exod. 20:3), where *'al* has the same meaning as in Gen. 11:28; 28:9; 31:50; etc. Yahweh is the sole object of Israelite worship. *Yahwe . . . yahwe* is the (discontinuous) predicate; *'ĕlōhēnū . . . 'eḥād* is the (discontinuous) subject: "Our one god is Yahweh, Yahweh." As a statement of the identity of "our only god," the sequence would be abnormal; but it is a grammatically acceptable answer to the implied question, "Who is our god?" The same construction is found in the cry of allegiance in Isaiah 33:22—"Our judge is Yahweh, our legislator is Yahweh, our king is Yahweh!"

Rule 7: When the predicate is a participle (phrase), the sequence is S–P in declarative clauses. Compare Rule 8.

Rule 7 is followed by 327 out of 355 declarative clauses with a participle as predicate. There are several factors involved in nonconformity to Rule 7.

(i) The participle may be not really verbal, but nominal in function. It has become a title or attribute, rather than a description of concrete current activity. This is why words like *rōṣēḥ*, "murderer," and *mᵉraggēl*, "spy," are classified in #94 and elsewhere as Ni, when Rule 3 is followed. This could explain Deut. 14:8 also. Compare Gen. 4:9. See p. 39.

(ii) The contrastive sequence P–S is preferred for precative clauses with Pti as P (Rule 8).

(iii) The abnormal sequence P–S may be a hint that the participle is wrongly identified; an infinitive absolute is a possible alternative. See Gen. 15:14; 31:20; 32:12; 42:23; Num. 10:29; 22:22; Deut. 19:6.

(iv) Another conceivable explanation lies in the adjectival character of passive participles, bringing them under Rule 3; but they show no marked preference for either sequence. Nor can P–S clauses be related to the use of a participle to indicate imminent future; again both sequences are used.

The sequence is the same for Rule 1 and Rule 7. This may account for the tendency to nominalize the participle by means of the definite article (##17, 48, 277, 326, 334, 343, 363).

There is a marked tendency to discontinuity when the predicate is a participle phrase. When the nucleus is <S–Pti>, discontinuity is achieved by having one of the modifiers of the participle in front of the subject—forty examples. When the nucleus is the abnormal <Pti–S>, discontinuity is achieved by having the modifiers of the participle after the subject. This occurs in nineteen of the twenty-eight P–S clauses. Indeed in only three of the nine P–S clauses without discontinuity (they are Gen. 15:14; Num. 14:14; Deut. 14:8) does the participle have a modifier that could show discontinuity. In other words, discontinuity is the rule for P–S participial clauses, when it is possible.

One effect of all this is that it is most unusual for a clause to begin with a participle. Only five independent clauses do it (##143, 153). Gen. 41:32 contains the only clause in the Pentateuch that seems to begin with *w-* + Pti. Independent participial clauses usually have *hinnē* as an auxiliary predicator. This makes *wmmhr* in Gen. 41:32 suspect. The explanation probably lies in the survival (masquerading as the participle) of *wm-mhr*, that is, the conjunction has enclitic *mem*,[13] and the "perfect" verb is used as a consecutive future—"and God will hasten to do it."

Rule 8: When the predicate is a participle (phrase), the sequence P–S is preferred in precative clauses. (See Table 6.)

Only passive participles are used in this way in our Corpus. The occurrence of eight precative clauses with sequence S–P (##474, 496) suggests that a declarative form may be used for blessing and cursing. Discontinuity is a common feature with both sequences. Rule 8 suggests that Gen. 31:52 is precative in contrast with Gen. 31:48, 50.

Numerals

There is no preferred sequence for clauses with a numeral (phrase) as predicate. About two-thirds (118) have S–P, one-third (61) P–S. About half are independent; the rest coordinated. No subordinated or nominalized clauses contain a numeral as predicate.

It is not possible to formulate rules; but some rough generalizations are possible. The sequence S–P is preferred in statements of population statistics (for example, ##45, 52), and of age (##192, 203, 247). #137 shows an exception to the latter. The sequence P–S is preferred in statements of specifications and dimensions (##122, 290, and others), and of definitions of weights and measures (##98, 114).

Partitive phrases

This predicate is always indefinite and follows Rule 3 in all six occurrences (##99, 123, 395, 473).

Rule 9: The sequence P–S is used when the subject of a declarative clause is an infinitive; the predicate is always an indefinite noun. Compare Rule 3. There are no exceptions.[14] The Corpus contains nine examples: ##129, 159, 299, 400, 428, 542.

Adverbs

The Corpus contains only fourteen clauses in which the predicate has been called an adverb. *'Aḥărannīt* occurs once, in #227; *kēn*, which occurs three times, could have been classed Ni; the other ten clauses contain *šām*. There are not enough data to lead to rules. Sequence S–P occurs four times; once in #227, which is circumstantial (Rule 5), three times (with *šām*) in #445. The ten clauses with sequence P–S include three with *kēn* (Rule 3) and seven with *šām*. Perhaps the sequence <*šām–S*> could be considered normal. Albrecht, however, again takes S–P as the norm, citing Num. 14:43 in support (p. 221). The sequence of P–S in Num. 13:22, normal in our view, he regards as an irregularity due to the long subject (p. 261).

Prepositional phrases

There are 258 declarative verbless clauses in the Pentateuch in which the predicate is a prepositional phrase. They are well distributed over the eight major clause types. 144 have sequence S–P; 114 have sequence P–S. No clear rules can be formulated for the normal use of one or other of these sequences.[15]

Several conditioning factors may be at work in this seemingly indeterminate situation; but a more comprehensive investigation involving more data is called for. Seventeen different prepositions are recognized in our Corpus. Some of them occur too rarely to permit normal patterns to be discovered. The preposition as such does not seem to correlate with sequence. While it is true that *b-* occurs more often in sequence S–P (41 times) than in P–S (28 times), and *l-* occurs more often in P–S (45 times) than S–P (22 times), others are equally divided—*'im,* 18 times in each sequence, *k-,* 9 times in each sequence.

The sequence S–P is preferred in precative clauses (Table 6); and the sequence S–P is favored in circumstantial clauses (compare Rule 5). But it does not follow that P–S is preferred for simple declarations.

To secure some kind of control by excluding any clauses that could be precative or circumstantial, subordinate and nominalized clauses give the best evidence, for they are exclusively declarative. Yet even here no clear picture emerges. The same items (that is, the same subject, the same predicate, and the same pattern in context) can be used in either sequence to yield clauses whose functions are indistinguishable. Compare: *'ăšer hannega' bō* (Lev. 13:46) with *'ăšer bō hannega'* (Lev. 13:45); or *'ăšer rûḥ 'ĕlōhîm bō* (Gen. 41:38) with *'ăšer bō rûḥ ḥayyîm* (Gen. 6:17). The clauses *weyahwe 'ittānû* (Num. 14:9) and *we'ittō 'ohŏlî'āb* (Exod. 38:23) both seem to be circumstantial. Another pair: *we'arba'-mē'ōt 'îš 'immō* (Gen. 32:7) and *we'immō 'arba'-mē'ōt 'îš* (Gen. 33:1)—both J!

Part III

The Corpus of Detailed Evidence

The Presentation of the Evidence in the Corpus

The weight of this study depends on the provision of ample evidence for valid inductions. This permits the conclusions to be tested independently by others and enables open questions to be pursued further. The Corpus serves as a concordance of verbless clause types, complete for the Pentateuch, selective for the rest of the Old Testament.

The clauses are classified by discourse function as declarative (##1-473), precative (##474-501) or interrogative (##502-555). Each of these three sets is further divided with reference to the exocentric function of the clause in context. Declarative clauses have four such relationships: independent (##1-174), coordinated (##175-321), subordinated (##322-439), and nominalized (##440-473).

Within each such subset two further sub-subsets are distinguished by their contrasting sequences S–P and P–S. Such sub-subsets constitute the major clause types, having the same nucleus sequence, the same exocentric function, and the same discourse function. There are eight such sub-subsets of declarative clauses, and four major types of precative clauses. Fuller details are given in the general Contents.

Further distinctions are made within each such sub-subset on the basis of differences of endocentric structure. Here the two chief features are the presence of discontinuity within the core and the presence or absence of marginal modifiers of the clause as a whole.

Tables 7-15 enable all clauses with the same kind of core to be readily found and compared.

Interrogative clauses are arranged differently, for reasons explained on page 38. Clauses in which an interrogative pronoun *mī* or *ma-* is the predicate are listed separately. The sequence is always P–S: ##502-519.[1] Clauses using other interrogatives follow, with nucleus S–P (##520-533, 553, 554) and then P–S (##534-552, 555).

Each entry (#) in the Corpus presents the evidence for one clause type in the narrowest sense. A typical example is quoted, with the reference. This is followed, under the rubric "other examples" by references to all other clauses of identical structure and function. The word "similarly" introduces references to additional clauses whose structural differences are trivial. Finally "compare" may adduce cross-references to clauses with similar or contrasting structures, including some from outside the Pentateuch. The similar clauses are included in the statistics; the compared clauses are not.

Occasionally an entry will be devoted to a clause type which happens not to occur in the Pentateuch; for example, #24*. For the sake of control these are not included in the statistics, and are marked with*.

The contents of the Corpus are summarized in Tables 7-15, which serve also as an index to all entries supplementing the Table of Contents.

##1-60. Independent declarative verbless clauses with core <S–P> and no margins

#1. <Pr–Np>
'ănī yahwe, "I am YHWH" (Exod. 6:2P, 6P, 8P, 29P; 12:12P; Lev. 18:5H, 6H, 21H; 19:12H, 14H, 16H, 18H, 28H, 30H, 32H, 37H; 21: 12H; 22:2H, 3H, 8H, 30H, 31H, 33H; 26:2H, 45H; Num. 3:13P, 41P, 45P). Other examples: Gen. 14:2P, 7P, 8P; 16:13J; 17:1P; 35:6P, 11P, 19E; 36:1P, 19P; 41:44E; 45:3E; 48:7E; Num. 33:36P; Deut. 4:48.

#2. <Pr–(Np <C> Np) >
hū' mōše we'ahărōn, "that is Moses and Aaron" (Exod. 6:27P).

#3. <Pr–P> In P Np is head of a complex noun-phrase.
Examples: Gen. 15:7J; 23:2P, 19P; 27:19P; 28:13J; 35:27P; 36:24P, 43P; 45:4J; Exod. 6:26P; 20:2E; 29:46P; Lev. 18:2H, 4H, 30H; 19:3H, 4H, 10H, 25H, 31H, 34H, 36H; 20:8H, 24H; 22:9H, 32–33H; 23:22H, 43H; 25:38H, 55H; 26:13H; Num. 10:10P; 15:41P, 41P; 26:9P; Deut. 5:6.

#4. <Pr–(N <Ct> Np) >
'ēlle benē 'ādā, "these are the sons of Adah" (Gen. 36:16P). Other examples: Gen. 6:9P; 11:10P; 36:19P; 37:2P; Exod. 6:14P, 15P. Albrecht (p. 220) considers the last example <P–S>.

#5. < (Pr <A> Pr) – (N <Ct> Np) >
'ēlle hēm benē yišmā''ēl, "these are the sons of Ishmael" (Gen. 25: 16P). Another example: Num. 3:33P. See p. 36.

#6. < (Num <M> Pr) – (N <Ct> Np) >
šelōšā 'ēlle benē-nōḥ, "these three are the sons of Noah" (Gen. 9: 19J). Other examples: Gen. 10:29J; 25:4L.

#7. <Pr–(N <Ct> N <Ct> Np) >
'ēlle 'allūpē benē-'ēśāw, "these are the chiefs of the sons of Esau" (Gen. 36:15P). Another example: Gen. 5:1P.

#8. <Pr–P> P is a complex phrase including (N <Ct> Np).

Examples: Gen. 26:24J; 35:26P; 36:5P, 12P, 17P, 18P; 46:15P, 18P, 22P, 25P; Lev. 7:35-36P; 23:4H, 37-38H; Num. 3:3P; 4:41P, 45P; 7:17P, 23P, 29P, 35P, 41P, 47P, 53P, 59P, 65P, 71P, 77P, 83P; 20:13P; 26:63P; 33:1P.

#9. <Pr–[(N <Ct> Np) <M> PpPh]>

'ēlle 'allūpē 'ĕlīpaz bᵉ'ereṣ 'ĕdōm, "these are the chiefs of Eliphaz in the land of Edom" (Gen. 36:16P). Other examples: Gen. 10:5P (see *Genesis:* Anchor Bible, p. 64), 20P, 31P, 32P; 36:17P, 43P; Num. 4:4P, 15P, 24P, 28P, 33P; 10:28P; 26:37P, 42P; 27:14P.

#10. <Pr–(Nd <A> Nd)>

hī' hā'īr haggᵉdōlā, "that is the chief city" (Gen. 10:12J).

#11. <Pr–P> P is a phrase with Nd as head.

'ēlle haṭṭᵉmē'īm lākem bᵉkol-haššāreṣ, "these are the unclean for you among all the swarmers" (Lev. 11:31P). Other examples: Gen. 31:13E; 46:3E; Exod. 12:42P; Lev. 14:54-57P.

#12. <Pr–(Nd <A> Nom)>

hū' hallehem 'ăšer nātan YHWH lākem lᵉ'oklā, "that is the bread that Yahweh has given you for food" (Exod. 16:15J). Other examples: Gen. 6:4L; 41:28E; Exod. 16:16L, 32L; 19:6E; 35:4P; Lev. 7:37P; 8: 5P; 9:6P; 11:2P; 17:2H; 26:46H; 27:34P; Num. 1:44P; 21:16E; 28:3P; 30:2P, 17P; 34:2P, 13P; 36:6P, 13P; Deut. 1:1; 4:45; 12:1; 14:4; 18:22; 34:4D.

#13. <Pr–(N <Ct> Nd)>

hū' yām hammelaḥ, "that is the sea of salt" (Gen. 14:3P). Other examples: Gen. 14:17P; Exod. 6:24P; 12:43P; Lev. 6:2P, 18P; 14:57P; Num. 1:16P; 7:2P; 26:7P.

#14. <(Pr <A> Pr)–(N <Ct> Nd)>

'ēlle hēm mišpᵉḥōt haggēršunnī, "these are the Gershunnite fratries" (Num. 3:21P). Another example: Num. 3:27P.

#15. <Pr–[(N <Ct> Nd) <M> PpPh]>

'ēlle 'allūpē hahōrī lᵉ'allūpēhem bᵉ'ereṣ śē'īr, "these are the Horite chiefs with reference to their chiefs in the land of Seir" (Gen. 36:30P). Other examples: Gen. 2:4P; 36:21P; Exod. 6:19P, 25P; Lev. 11:46-47P; 12:7P; 13:59P; Num. 7:88P.

#16. <Pr–[(N <Ct> Nd) <A> Nom]>

'ēlle šᵉmōt hā'ănāšim 'ăšer-šālaḥ mōše lātūr 'et-hā'āreṣ, "these are the names of the men whom Moses sent to explore the land" (Num.

13:16P). Other examples: Gen. 9:12P, 17P; Exod. 38:21P; Lev. 15:32P; Num. 4:37P; 5:29P; 6:21P; 19:2P; 31:21P; Deut. 28:69.

#17. <Pr–PtdPh>

hū' hassōbēb 'ēt kol-'ereṣ kūš, "this is the one that winds through all the land of Kush" (Gen. 2:13J). Other examples: Gen. 2:11J, 14J; 42:6J; Exod. 6:27P; Lev. 6:2P; Num. 7:2P.

#18. <Pr–Nom>

zō't 'ăšer lalwiyyīm, "this is what concerns the Levites" (Num. 8: 24P). Other examples: Gen. 42:14E; 49:8L (Nom=Ø); Exod. 16:23J; 30:13P (Nom=Ø); Lev. 10:3P; 14:32P; Num. 34:29P.

#19. <Pr–Ns>

hū' 'ădōnī, "he is my master" (Gen. 24:65J). Other examples: Gen. 40:12E, 18E; Exod. 15:2; Deut. 10:21.

#20. <Pr–P> P is a phrase with Ns as head.

hī' śimlātō lĕ'ōrō, "it is his clothing for his skin" (Exod. 22:26C). Other examples: Gen. 17:10P; 20:13E; 27:32J (compare 27:19J); Exod. 3:15E; Num. 18:20P.

#21. < (Pr <A> Pr) – (Ns <A> Np) >

'attā ze bᵉnī 'ēśāw, "you are my son Esau (?)" (Gen. 27:24J). Compare Gen. 27:21J.

#22. <Pr–[(N <Ct> Ns) <A> (N <Ct> Np)]>

'ānōkī 'ĕlōhē 'ābīkā 'ĕlōhē 'abrāhām 'ĕlōhē yiṣḥāq wĕ'lōhē ya'ăqōb, "I am the god of your father, the god of Abraham, Isaac, and Jacob" (Exod. 3:6E).

#23. <Pr–Pti (Ph) >

hī' mūṣē't, "she is being brought out" (Gen. 38:25L). Other examples: Gen. 42:35E; 49:29P; Deut. 2:4, 18; 5:5; 9:1; 20:3; 29:9. Compare Gen. 15:1J and Num. 9:7 in #25. Similarly Exod. 12:33L.

#24.* <Pr–Ni>

'ănī ri'šōn, "I am first" (Isa. 44:6). Another example: Isa. 48:12.

#25. <Pr–P> P is a phrase with Ni as head.

'ănahnū ṭᵉmā'īm lᵉnepeš 'ādām, "we are defiled by a human corpse" (Num. 9:7P). Other examples: Gen. 15:1J; Num. 13:2P; Deut. 3:5.

#26. <Pr–(N <Ct> Ni) >

'attem 'am-qᵉšē-'ōrep, "you are a tough-necked people" (Exod. 33: 5E). Other examples: Gen. 42:13E; Exod. 25:36P; 37:22P; Num. 28: 14P.

#27. <Pr–PpPh>
'ănōkī badderek, "I am on the road" (Gen. 24:27J). Another example: Gen. 40:16E. Compare II Sam. 13:30.

#28.* <Np–Ns>
yahwe šᵉmō, "YHWH is his name" (Exod. 15:3). But <P–S> is preferred; see #119 and p. 41.

#29. <Np–PtiPh>
'ămālēq yōšēb bᵉ'ereṣ hannegeb, "Amalek lives in the Negeb land" (Num. 13:29J). Other examples: Gen. 31:50E; Num. 11:27J; 24:8J.

#30. <Np–Ni>
yahwe 'eḥād, "YHWH is one" (Deut. 6:4). Another example: Gen. 49:5L. Compare I Kings 4:20.

#31. <Np–(Ni <A> Ni)>
nōḥ 'īš ṣaddīq, "Noah is a righteous man" (Gen. 6:9P). Other examples: Gen. 49:21L, 27L.

#32. <Np–(N <Ct> Ni)>
šēm ben mᵉ'at šānā, "Shem is one hundred years old" (Gen. 11:10P). Other examples: Exod. 15:3; Deut. 33:22, 23.

#33. <Np–(N <Ct> Ni) Ph>
yiśśā(s)kār ḥămōr gārem rōbēṣ bēn hammišpᵉtāyim, "Issachar is a strong ass, crouching between the sheepfolds" (Gen. 49:14L [RSV]). Another example: Num. 14:18P (=Nah. 1:3). See p. 44.

#34. <Np–PpPh>
yahwe 'ĕlōhāyw 'immō, "YHWH his god is with him" (Num. 23:21E). Another example: Gen. 12:8J.

#35. <(N <Ct> Np)–Np>
bᵉkōr ya'ăqōb rᵉ'ūbēn, "Jacob's firstborn is Reuben" (Gen. 46:8P). Other examples: Gen. 10:2P, 22P; 11:29J; 35:23P, 24P; 36:15P; 46:19P; Exod. 6:14P, 17P; Num. 26:19P. See p. 41.

#36. <(N <Ct> [Np <C> Np]–(Md <M> Ni)>
za'ăqat sᵉdōm wa'ămōrā kī-rabbā, "the outcry of Sodom and Gomorrah is very great" (Gen. 18:20J). Compare Ezek. 9:9.

#37. <Nd–(N <Ct> Np)>
haqqōl qōl ya'ăqōb, "the voice is Jacob's voice" (Gen. 27:22J).

#38. <Nd–Ns>
habbānōt bᵉnōtay, "the daughters are my daughters" (Gen. 31:43E).

#39. < (Nd <A> Nd) –PtiPh>

haggal hazze ʿēd bēnī ūbēnᵉkā hayyōm, "this heap is witnessing between me and you today" (Gen. 31:48J). Compare II Sam. 17:29.

#40. <Nd– (Md <M> Ni) >

(*ʾet-*) *hāʾōr kī ṭōb,* "the light is so good" (Gen. 1:4P). Compare Jos. 4:24. Similarly Exod. 12:2P.

#41. <Nd–PpPh>

hannistārōt lᵉyahwe ʾĕlōhēnū, "the secrets belong to YHWH our god" (Deut. 29:28). Another example: Num. 5:8P.

#42. < (N <Ct> Nd) –Np>

šēm hāʾeḥād pīšōn, "the name of the first is Pishon" (Gen. 2:11J). Other examples: Gen. 4:19L; 10:25J; 29:16L; Num. 11:26J.

#43. <[(N <Ct> N <Ct> Nd) <M> Md]–PtiPh>

kol-ʿammūdē heḥāṣēr sābīb mᵉḥuššāqīm kesep, "all the posts around the court are banded with silver" (Exod. 27:17P).

#44. <[(N <Ct> Nd) <C> Ns]–Ni>

wāwē hāʿammūdīm waḥăšūqēhem kāsep, "the hooks and bands of the posts are silver" (Exod. 27:10P, 11P; 38:10P, 11P, 12P, 17P). Another example: Exod. 38:16P. Compare Gen. 31:12E.

#45. < (N <Ct> Nd) Ph–Num>

kol-hannepeš lᵉbēt-yaʿăqōb habbāʾā miṣraymā šibʿīm, "all the persons of Jacob's family who came to Egypt are seventy" (Gen. 46:27P). Other examples: Exod. 26:2P, 8P; 27:18P; 36:9P, 15P; Num. 2:9P, 16P, 24P, 31P; 3:39P; 26:43P; 35:7P.

#46. < (N <Ct> Nd) –PpPh>

mahănē halwiyyīm bᵉtōk hammahănōt, "the camp of the Levites is in the middle of the camps" (Num. 2:17P).

#47. <Ns–Np>

šimkā yaʿăqōb, "your name is Jacob" (Gen. 35:10P).

#48. <Ns–PtdPh>

ʿēnēkem hārōʾōt ʾēt ʾăšer ʿāśā yahwe bᵉbaʿal pᵉʿōr, "your eyes are the ones that saw what YHWH did at Baal-Peor" (Deut. 4:3). Another example: Deut. 3:21.

#49. <Ns–PtiPh>

ʾădōnī yōdēʿ kī hayᵉlādīm rakkīm, "my lord knows that the children are frail" (Gen. 33:13J).

56

#50. <Ns–Ni>
'ābīnū zāqēn, "our father is old" (Gen. 19:31L) . Other examples:
Exod. 26:32P, 37P; 27:17P; 36:36P; 38:19P. Compare Isa. 56:10; Jer.
50:34.

#51. <Ns–(N <Ct> Ni) >
'ănābēmō 'inn^{e}bē-rōš, "their grapes are grapes of poison" (Deut.
32:32) . Compare Isa. 22:2.

#52. <Ns–Num>
'ammūdēhem 'ăśārā, "their posts are ten" (Exod. 27:12P) . Other
examples: Exod. 27:14P, 15P, 16P; 38:10P, 11P, 12P, 14P, 15P; twelve
examples in Num. 1; Num. 3:22P; twelve examples in Num. 7 (all P) .

#53. < (N <Ct> Ns) –PtiPh>
d^{e}mē 'āhīkā ṣō'ăqīm 'ēlay min hā'ădāmā, "your brother's blood is
crying to me from the ground" (Gen. 4:10L) . See Genesis: Anchor
Bible, p. 29.

#54. < (N <Ct> N <Ct> Ns) –Num>
y^{e}mē š^{e}nē m^{e}gūray š^{e}lōšīm ūm^e'at šānā, "the period of the years
of my sojournings is one hundred thirty years" (Gen. 47:9P) .

#55. < (N <Ct> Ns) –PpPh>
kol-q^{e}dōšāyw b^{e}yādekā, "all his holy ones are in your hand" (Deut.
33:3) . Another example: Gen. 27:27J.

#56. <Ni–(Md <M> Ni) >
m^{e}nūhā kī ṭōb, "the resting place is so good" (Gen. 49:15L) .

#57. <Ni–PpPh>
mūm bō, "a defect is in it" (Lev. 21:21H) . Other examples: Lev.
22:25H; Gen. 43:28J.

#58. < (N <Ct> Ni) –Num>
kol-nepeš šib'ā, "all persons are seven" (Gen. 46:25P) . Other examples: Gen. 46:15P, 22P, 26P.

#59. < (N <Ct> Ni) –PpPh>
qōl milhāmā b^{e}mahăne, "a noise of battle is in the camp" (Exod.
32:17J) . Compare Isa. 1:5.

#60. <NumPh–PpPh>
š^{e}nē gōyīm b^{e}biṭnēk, "two nations are in your abdomen" (Gen.
25:23J) . Other examples: Exod. 26:21P; 36:26P; Lev. 27:16P.

##61-73. Independent declarative verbless clauses with core <S–P> plus margins

#61. <Pr–(N <Ct> Np) > + PpPh

hū' 'ăbī-mō'āb 'ad-hayyōm, "he is the ancestor of Moab until today" (Gen. 19:37L). Other examples: Gen. 19:38L; 35:20E.

#62. <Pr–(Md <M> [Pti <Ct> Np]) >

'attā 'attā berūk yahwe, "you are now the one blessed by YHWH" (Gen. 26:29J).

#63. <Pr–Nd> + Cl

zō't hattōrā 'ādām kī-yāmūt be'ōhel, "this is the rule when a man dies in camp" (Num. 19:14P).

#64. <Pr–(Ns [Voc] <A> Nom) >

'ēlle 'ĕlōheykā yiśrā'ēl 'ăšer he'ĕlūkā mē'ereṣ miṣrayim, "these are your gods, Israel, who brought you up from the land of Egypt" (Exod. 32:4E, 8E).

#65. Exc + <Pr–PtiPh>

re'ē 'ānōkī nōtēn lipnēkem hayyōm berākā ūqelālā, "behold, I am putting before you today blessing and curse" (Deut. 11:26). Another example: Exod. 33:12J.

#66. IfPh + <Pr–Ni>

bešaggām hū' bāśār, "in erring he is flesh" (Gen. 6:3L). This is uncertain.

#67. <Pr–[Md]–(Ni <M> PpPh) >

zō't happa'am 'eṣem mē'ăṣāmay ūbāśār mibbeśārī, "this at last is bone from my bones and flesh from my flesh" (Gen. 2:23J).

#68. Adv + <Pr–PpPh>

ze 'eśrīm šānā 'ānōkī 'immāk, "now I've been with you twenty years" (Gen. 31:38J). Compare #70.

#69. Adv + <Np–PtiPh>

'ăbāl śārā 'ištekā yōledet lekā bēn, "notwithstanding, Sarah your wife is bearing you a son" (Gen. 17:19P).

#70. Adv + <Np–PpPh>

ze 'arbā'īm šānā yahwe 'ĕlōheykā 'immāk, "now YHWH your god has been with you forty years" (Deut. 2:7). Compare #68.

#71. Adv + <[(N <Ct> Np) <A> Ns]–PpPh> + PpPh

tāmīd 'ēnē yahwe 'ĕlōheykā bāh mērē'šīt haššānā we'ad 'ăḥărīt šānā, "always the eyes of YHWH your god are on it, from the beginning of the year until the end of the year" (Deut. 11:12).

#72. <Ns–[Voc]–PtiPh>
y^emīn^ekā yahwe ne'dārī bakkōḥ, "your right hand, YHWH, is glorious in power" (Exod. 15:6).

#73. Neg + <Ns–PpPh>
biltī 'ăḥīkem 'itt^ekem, "your brother is not with you" (Gen. 43:3J, 5J).

#74-80. Independent declarative verbless clauses with core <S...–P...S>

#74. <Pr...–(N <Ct> Np) ...List>
'ēlle b^enē-'ēṣer bilhan w^eza'āwān wa'ăqān, "these are the sons of Ezer—Bilhan and Zaavan and Akan" (Gen. 36:27P). Other examples: Gen. 36:10P, 15P, 20P, 28P; Lev. 6:13P; Num. 26:30-32P, 35P, 42P, 58P.

#75. <Pr...–(N <Ct> Np) ...Num>
kol-'ēlle šibṭē yiśrā'ēl š^enēm 'āśār, "all these are the tribes of Israel —twelve" (Gen. 49:28L). Other examples: Num. 2:32P; 26:18P, 22P, 25P, 34P, 37P, 41P, 50P, 51P.

#76. <Pr...–(N <Ct> Nd) ...List>
Examples: Gen. 36:29P; Num. 7:84-88P; 34:17P.

#77. < (Pr <A> Pr)...–(N <Ct> Nd) ...List>
Example: Num. 3:20-33P; the distributive list is spread through the paragraph. Compare Gen. 46:8-27.

#78. <Pr...–(N <Ct> Nd) ...Num>
Examples: Num. 26:14P, 27P.

#79. <Pr...–(N <Ct> N <Ct> Ns) ...List>
Example: Exod. 6:14P.

#80. <[(Ni <C> Ni) <A> Ni]...–PpPh ...<C> (Ni <M> If) >
gam-teben gam-mispō' rab 'immānū gam-māqōm lālūn, "with us are both straw and abundant food and a place to sleep" (Gen. 24:25J).

#81-83. Independent declarative verbless clauses with core <P... S–...P>

#81. <Md... Pr–...Pti>
'et-hā'ĕlōhīm 'ănī yārē', "I reverence God" (Gen. 42:18E). Other examples: Gen. 16:8J; 37:16J; 38:25L; 41:9E; Exod. 11:4J; 13:4L; 17:9J; 32:15E; 18J; Lev. 21:9H; Deut. 4:12; 9:5. Compare II Sam. 13:4.

#82. <Md... Np–...PtiPh>

hayyōm hazze yahwe 'ĕlōheykā mᵉṣawwᵉkā la'ăśōt 'et-haḥuqqīm hā'ēlle wᵉ'et-hammišpāṭīm, "today YHWH your god commands you to perform these statutes and decisions" (Deut. 26:16).

#83. <Md... (N <Ct> Np)–...Pti>

kēn bᵉnōt ṣᵉlophād dōbᵉrōt, "the daughters of Zelophehad speak correctly" (Num. 27:7P). Another example: Num. 36:5P.

##84-88. Independent declarative verbless clauses with core <SSus, SRes–P>

#84. <NpSus,Pr–Np>

'ēśāw hū' 'ĕdōm, "Esau, he is Edom" (Gen. 36:8P).

#85. <NdSus,Pr–Nd>

hā'īš 'ăšer-yibḥar yahwe hū' haqqādōš, "the man whom YHWH chooses, he is the holy one" (Num. 16:7P). Another example: Gen. 24:43 f.

#86. <NpSus,Pr–Ns> + [Mg]

yahwe hū' naḥălātō ka'ăšer dibber-lō, "YHWH, he is his inheritance, as he told him" (Deut. 18:2). Another example: Deut. 10:9. Similarly Lev. 23:2H. Compare Ezek. 27:21.

#87. <NpSus,Pr–PtiPh>

yahwe 'ĕlōheykā hū' 'ōbēr lᵉpāneykā, "YHWH your god, he is crossing in front of you" (Deut. 31:3). Another example: De 31:3.

#88. <NdPhSus,(N <Ct> Ni)–Num>

kol-hannepeš habbā'ā lᵉya'ăqōb miṣraymā ... kol-nepeš šiššīm wāšēš, "all the persons who came to Egypt belonging to Jacob ... all persons are sixty-six" (Gen. 46:26P).

#89. Independent declarative verbless clauses with core <PSus,S– PRes>

#89. <NSus,Ni–PpPh>

'aškᵉlōt mᵉrōrōt lāmō, "clusters, bitter things are theirs" (Deut. 32:32). Other examples: Deut. 33:2, 17. It is problematical whether the suspended noun predicate is resumed as a pronoun suffix in the predicate. The analysis of Deut. 32:32 must overcome the discord in gender. RSV "their clusters are bitter" supposes *'aškᵉlōt ... lāmō* is a discontinuous equivalent of *'aškᵉlōtēhem,* with core <S...–P...S>. RSV Deut. 33:17 supports the analysis adopted here. In Deut. 33:2 MT reads *mīmīmō,* "from his right hand"; but *m-* is probably enclitic (not plural!) with preceding *qdš[m].*

##90-131. Independent declarative verbless clauses with core <P–S> and no margins

#90. < (N <Ct> Np) –Pr>

'ebed 'abrāhām 'ānōkī, "I am Abraham's slave" (Gen. 24:34J).
Other examples: Gen. 32:3E; Exod. 8:15P. Similarly Num. 1:16P.
Compare Judg. 12:4.

#91. < (N <Ct> Nd) –Pr>

ḥaṭṭa't haqqāhāl hū', "it is the assembly's sin offering" (Lev. 4:21P).
Other examples: Lev. 13:23P, 28P, 30P.

#92. <Ns–Pr>

'āḥī hū', "he is my brother" (Gen. 20:5E, 13E). Other examples:
Gen. 12:12J, 13J, 19J; 20:2E, 5E; 24:60E; 26:7L, 9L; Lev. 15:3P; 18:
7H, 11H, 14H. Compare Ugaritic *'bdk an* (67:II:12) ; Jos. 9:11; Judg.
8:19; 9:3; II Kings 10:5.

#93. < (N <Ct> Ns) –Pr>

'ēšet binkā hī', "she is your son's wife" (Lev. 18:15H). Other examples: Lev. 18:8H, 12H, 16H; Num. 1:16P. Compare Mari *warad
bēliya anāku* (André Finet, *L'Accadien des lettres de Mari* [Brussels,
1956], p. 208).

#94. <Ni–Pr>

ṭāmē' hū', "he is unclean" (Lev. 13:36P). Other examples: Gen.
42:9E, 11E, 13J, 14E, 31E; Exod. 29:14P; 30:32P; Lev. 2:6P, 15P; 4:
24P; 5:9P, 12P, 19P; 7:5P; 11:13P, 35P, 37P; 13:6P, 8P, 13P, 15P, 17P,
22P, 25P, 30P, 37P, 39P, 39P, 40P, 40P, 41P, 44P, 46P, 51P, 55P;
14:44P; 15:25P; 18:17H, 17H, 22H, 23H; 23:36H; 25:11H; Num.
14:28P; 18:17P; 19:9P, 20P; 35:16P, 17P, 18P, 21P. Compare II Sam.
1:8; 11:5.

The question *mān hū' (=ma-hū'),* "what is it?" (Exod. 16:15J)
was apparently transferred, perhaps by deliberate paronomasia rather
than through misconstruction of obsolete *mān* to clause category #94.
So *mān* becomes a noun—"it is *man*." Compare Exod. 16:31L. The
normal sequence <P–S> assisted this.

#95. < (Ni <A> Ni) –Pr>

'ēl qannā' hū', "he is a passionate god" (Exod. 34:14J). Compare
Jos. 24:19E. Another example: Lev. 13:44P. Compare Jos. 17:17; I
Sam. 1:15; Jer. 4:22.

#96. < (Ni <C> Ni) –Pr>

ṣaddīq weyāšār hū', "he is just and right" (Deut. 32:4).

#97. < (N <Ct> Ni) –Pr>

bigdē-qōdeš hēm, "they are holy garments" (Lev. 16:4P). Other examples: Lev. 6:18P, 22P; 7:1P, 6P; 13:3P, 20P, 25P, 27P, 49P; 14:13P; Num. 5:18P. Similarly Exod. 29:18P; Num. 25:15L. Compare II Sam. 1:13.

#98. <Num–Pr>

'esrīm gērā hū', "it is twenty gerahs" (Num. 18:16P).

#99. <Part–Pr>

miyyaldē hā'ibrīm ze, "this is one of the Hebrew children" (Exod. 2:6E). See p. 22.

#100. <PpPh–Pr>

lī hū', "it is mine" (Exod. 13:2L). Another example: Gen. 29:4E.

#101. < (Neg <M> PpPh) –Pr>

lō' baššāmayim hī', "it is not in heaven" (Deut. 30:12).

#102. <Nom–Np>

hēnīqā bānīm sārā, "Sarah is one who suckled a son" (Gen. 21:7J). The sequence is abnormal for a verbal clause, where subject precedes object. The nominalizer is zero, either archaic or a signal of indefiniteness. We read *bn<y>m* as singular plus enclitic *mem.*

#103.* <PtiPh–Np>

niṣṣāb lārīb yahwe, "YHWH stands to litigate" (Isa. 3:13).

#104. <Ns–Np>

beni bekōrī yisrā'ēl, "Israel is my son, my firstborn" (Exod. 4:22L). Another example: Exod. 15:2. Compare Isa. 12:2.

#105. <Ni–Np>

me'ōnā 'ĕlōhē qedem, "the eternal God is a dwelling place" (Deut. 33:27; compare Ps. 74:12). Compare Esther 7:6 (but see RSV); II Chron. 12:6.

#106. < (Neg <M> Ni) –Np>

lō' 'īš 'ēl, "God is not a man" (Num. 23:19E). Compare I Sam. 15: 29.

#107. < (N <Ct> Ni) –Np>

gūr 'aryē yehūdā, "Judah is a lion cub" (Gen. 49:9L). Another example: Num. 24:20J. Compare I Kings 20:28; Isa. 40:28; Jer. 46:20; Hos. 10:1.

#108.* <Ni–[(N <Ct> Np) <A> Nd] >

qārōb yōm yahwe haggādōl, "YHWH's great day is near" (Zeph. 1:14). Compare II Kings 20:19; Isa. 39:8.

#109. \<Np–Nd\>

yahwe haṣṣaddīq, "the one in the right is YHWH" (Exod. 9:27J).
Translations like RSV "the Lord is in the right" have missed the
point. The question is, "Who is in the right?" so *haṣṣaddīq* is the subject of the answer. See pp. 21, 42.

#110.* \<Ni–Nd\>

ṭōb haddābār, "the word is good" (I Kings 2:38 [=18:24]). Compare
Hos. 9:7.

#111. \< (Ni \<A\> Ni) –Nd\>

ṣāraʿat mamʾeret hannegaʿ, "the lesion is malignant leprosy" (Lev.
13:51P). Other examples, with exclamatory *ma-:* Gen. 28:17E; Deut.
29:23.

#112. \<Ni–(Nd \<A\> Nom) \>

ṭōb-haddābār ʾăšer-dibbartā laʿăśōt, "the thing that you have said
to do is good" (Deut. 1:14). Another example: Deut. 1:25. Similarly
Exod. 18:17E. Compare II Chron. 9:5; with negation I Sam. 26:16; II
Sam. 17:7.

#113. \< (N \<Ct\> Ni) –Nd\>

ṭūr ʾōdem piṭdā ūbāreqet haṭṭūr hāʾehād, "the first row is a row
of sardius, topaz, and carbuncle" (Exod. 28:17P; 39:10P). Compare
II Kings 19:3 (=Isa. 37:3); Zeph. 1:15.

#114. \<Num–Nd\>

ʿeśrīm gērā haššeqel, "the shekel is twenty gerahs" (Exod. 30:13P;
Num. 3:47P). Another example: Num. 11:21J.

#115. \<Adv–Nd\>

šām habbedōlaḥ weʾeben haššōham, "bdellium and onyx stone are
there" (Gen. 2:12J).

#116. \<PpPh–Nd\>

lānū hammāyim, "the water is ours" (Gen. 26:20L).

#117. \<Num–(N \<Ct\> Nd) \>

šelōš mēʾōt ʾammā ʾōrek hattēbā, "the length of the ark is three
hundred cubits" (Gen. 6:15P). Other examples: Exod. 26:16P; 36:21P.

#118. \<PpPh–(N \<Ct\> Nd) \>

lō mišpaṭ habbekōrā, "the firstborn's portion is his" (Deut. 21:17).
Other examples: Lev. 23:34H; Num. 3:21P, 33P; 26:29P.

#119. \<Np–Ns\>

yahwe šemō, "His name is YHWH" (Exod. 15:3).

#120. <Ni–Ns>

*'ayil 'ăšāmō, "his guilt offering is a ram" (Lev. 19:21H). Other examples: Num. 24:21J; Deut. 26:5; 29:22; 33:25. Compare I Sam. 9:10; Isa. 50:8; with apposition Jer. 9:7; Dan. 11:5; with coordination Isa. 41:29.

#121. < (N <Ct> Ni) –Ns>

kᵉlē ḥāmās mᵉkārōtēkem, "their swords (?) are weapons of violence" (Gen. 49:5L). Another example: Gen. 47:3J. Compare I Kings 20:23; Isa. 6:13; 13:8; Mic. 7:6.

#122. <Num–Ns>

tēša' 'ammōt 'orkāh, "its length is nine cubits" (Deut. 3:11). Other examples: Gen. 6:15P; 24:22E, 22E; 42:13E; Exod. 25:10P, 17P, 23P; 27:1P (normalized to Exod. 38:1); 28:16P; 30:2P; 37:1P, 6P, 10P, 25P; 38:1P; 39:9P.

#123. <Part–Ns>

mimmennū qarnōtāyw, "its horns are part of it" (Exod. 30:2P).

#124. < (Neg <M> Adv) – (Ns <A> Np) >

lō'-kēn 'abdī mōše, "my servant Moses is not so" (Num. 12:7J). Compare II Sam. 20:21.

#125. <PpPh–Ns>

lᵉlēwī. . . tummeykā, "your tummīm are for Levi" (Deut. 33:8).

#126. <Np–(N <Ct> Ns) >

ya'ăqōb ḥebel naḥălātō, "his patrimonial allotment is Jacob" (Deut. 32:9). Compare #86 and Jer. 10:16.

#127. <PpPh–Ni>

bayyōm hārī'šōn šabbātōn, "a rest-day is on the first day" (Lev. 23: 39H). Other examples: Exod. 27:19P; Lev. 23:5H, Deut. 32:35.

#128. <PpPh–(N <Ct> Ni) >

bayyōm haššᵉbī'ī miqrā'-qōdeš, "a holy meeting is on the seventh day" (Num. 28:18P). Other examples: Lev. 23:8P, 35P.

#129. < (Neg <M> Ni) –IfPh>

lō'-ṭōb hĕyōt hā'ādām lᵉbaddō, "for the man to be alone is not good" (Gen. 2:18J). Other examples: Gen. 29:7L; Deut. 1:6; 2:3.

#130. <Num–PpPh>

'aḥad 'āśār yōm mēḥōrēb derek har-śē'īr 'ad qādēš barnē', "from Horeb to Kadesh-Barnea by Mount Seir highway is eleven days" (Deut. 1:2).

#131. <PpPh–PpPh>
kākem kaggēr, "the alien is like you" (Num. 15:15P). Other examples: Gen. 18:25J; Lev. 7:7P.

#132-140. Independent declarative verbless clauses with core <P–S> plus margins

#132.* Exc + < (N <Ct> Np)–Pr>
'ak melek-yiśrā'ēl hū', "surely he is the king of Israel" (I Kings 22: 32).

#133. Exc + < (Ns <C> Ns–Pr>
'ak 'aṣmī ūbᵉśārī 'āttā, "surely you are my bone and my flesh" (Gen. 29:14J; compare #67 and II Sam. 5:1; 19:13, 14). Compare Isa. 19:11.

#134. PpPh + <Ni–Pr>
'ad-yᵉrēkāh 'ad-pirḥāh miqšā hī', "from its base to its petals it is hammered work" (Num. 8:4P). Another example: Num. 12:7J.

#135. Mod + <Ni–Pr>
'ūlay mišge hū', "perhaps it is a mistake" (Gen. 43:12J).

#136. Exc + Voc + < (Neg <M> [N <Ct> Ni])–Pr> + PpPh
bī 'ădōnay lō' 'īš dᵉbārīm 'ānōkī gam mittᵉmōl gam miššilšōm gam mē'āz dabberkā 'el-'abdekā, "please, my lord, I am not a speaker, neither yesterday, nor the day before, nor since you spoke to me" (Exod. 4:10E).

#137. <Num–Pr> + Adv
ben-mē'ā wᵉ'eśrīm šānā 'ānōkī hayyōm, "I am one hundred and twenty years old today" (Deut. 31:2). Compare (with S=Np and Adv=IfPh) Jos. 14:7; II Sam. 5:4; 19:36; I Kings 14:21; II Kings 8:26; 12:1; 16:2; 21:1, 19; 22:1; 23:31, 36; 24:8, 18; Jer. 52:1; II Chr. 12:13; 21:5; 22:2; 24:1; 26:3; 27:1; 28:1; 33:1; 21; 34:1; 36:2, 5, 9, 11.

#138. Cl + <PpPh–Pr>
'im-šōr 'im-śe lᵉyahwe hū', "whether ox or sheep, it is YHWH's" (Lev. 27:26P).

#139. Exc + < (Ni <A> [Ni <C> Ni])–(Nd <A> Nd <A> Nd) >
raq 'am-ḥākām wᵉnābōn haggōy haggādōl hazze, "surely this great nation is a wise and discerning people" (Deut. 4:6). Compare Isa. 40:7.

#140. Exc + <PpPh–Ni>
hē' lākem zera', "well, you have seed" (Gen. 47:23J).

65

##141-159. Independent declarative verbless clauses with core <P...-S...P> and no margins

#141. < (N <Ct> Np)...-Pr ...PpPh>

nᵉśî' 'ĕlōhîm 'attā bᵉtōkēnū, "you are a prince of God in our midst" (Gen. 23:6P). Similarly Gen. 24:24J; compare Gen. 24:47J.

#142. <Ns...-Pr ... Nom>

'ăbāday hēm 'ăšer-hōṣē'tī 'ōtām mē'ereṣ miṣrāyim, "they are my slaves whom I brought from the land of Egypt" (Lev. 25:55H). Another example: Gen. 48:9E. Similarly Deut. 21:20.

#143. <Pti...-Pr ...PpPh>

nᵉbūkîm hēm bā'āreṣ, "they are entangled in the land" (Exod. 14:3L). Other examples: Gen. 31:5E; Num. 10:29J.

#144. <Ni...-Pr ...<A> Ni>

nirpîm 'attem nirpîm, "you are utterly idle" (Exod. 5:17J). RSV "you are idle, you are idle" supposes elliptical omission of a second *'attem*. Identification of elative repetition leads to recognition of the discontinuous predicate *nirpîm... nirpîm*. Compare *nᵉtūnîm nᵉtūnîm* in Num. 3:9. Similarly Gen. 32:19E; 42:13J/E; Lev. 1:13P, 17P. Compare Isa. 19:11.

#145. <Ni...-Pr ...<M> PpPh>

pesaḥ hū' lᵉyahwe, "it is a passover for YHWH" (Exod. 12:11P). Other examples: Exod. 12:2P; 29:18P, 25P; Lev. 8:21P, 21P, 28P, 28P; 11:4P, 5P, 6P, 7P, 8P, 28P, 38P; 13:55P; 23:3H; Num. 6:20P; Deut. 14:1, 7, 8, 10, 32:40. Compare Jos. 9:22; Judg. 17:9; I Sam. 24:18; Jer. 4:22.

#146. < (Ni <A> Ni)...-Pr ...<M> PpPh>

'ēbel-kābēd ze lᵉmiṣrāyim, "this is heavy mourning of Egypt" (Gen. 50:11J). Other examples: Lev. 13:11P; 14:44P; Num. 3:9P.

#147. <Ni <C> Ni)...-Pr ...<M> PpPh>

gēr-wᵉtōšāb 'ānōkî 'immākem, "I am an alien and a resident among you" (Gen. 23:4P).

#148. < (N <Ct> Ni)...-Pr ...<M> PpPh>

qōdeš-qodāšîm hū' lᵉyahwe, "it is most holy for YHWH" (Exod. 30:10P). Other examples: Exod. 12:27L; Lev. 6:10P; 16:31P; 23:32H. Similarly Exod. 12:42P; Num. 18:19P.

#149. < ([N <Ct> Ni] <M> [PpPh...-Pr ...<C> PpPh]) >

qōdeš qodāšîm lᵉkā hū' ūlᵉbāneykā, "it is most holy for you and for your sons" (Num. 18:9P).

#150. <Num...–Pr ...<A> (Ni <A> [N <Ct> Ns]) >

šᵉnēm-ʿāśār 'ănaḥnū 'aḥim bᵉnē 'ābīnū, "we are twelve brothers, sons of our father" (Gen. 42:32E).

#151. <(N <Ct> Ni)...–Np...<A> [(N <Ct> Ni) <M> PpPh]>

bēn pōrāt yōsēp bēn pōrāt ʿălē-ʿāyin, "son of a wild colt is Joseph, son of a wild colt beside a spring" (Gen. 49:22L).

#152.* <Ni...–(N <Ct> Np) ...<M> PpPh>

ṭōbā ʿăṣat ḥūšay hā'arki mēʿăṣat 'ăḥītōpel, "the advice of Hushay the Arkite is better than the advice of Ahithophel" (II Sam. 17:14).

#153. <Pti...–Nd ...IfPh>

marbīm hāʿām lᵉhābi' middē hā'ăbōdā lammᵉlā'kā 'ăšer ṣiwwā yahwe laʿăśōt 'ōtāh, "the people excel in bringing enough for the work which YHWH commanded to do" (Exod. 36:5P). Similarly Exod. 26:5P.

#154. <Ni...–Nd ...<M> PpPh>

rabbīm haggōyim hā'ēlle mimmennī, "these nations are more numerous than I" (Deut. 7:17). Compare: Judg. 7:2; Jer. 17:9.

#155. <Ni...–Ns ...<M> PpPh>

*ḥaklīlī *ʿēnēmō miyyāyin,* "[his] eyes are more sparkling than wine" (Gen. 49:12L). Another example: Gen. 4:13J.

#156. < (N <Ct> Ni)...–Ns ...<C> [(N <Ct> Ni) <A> Ni]>

ḥămat tannīnīm yēnām wᵉrō'š pᵉtānīm 'akzār, "their wine is serpent poison and cruel asp venom" (Deut. 32:33).

#157.* <Num...–Ns ...Ni>

šᵉnēm ʿăśār ʿăbādeykā 'aḥīm, "your servants are twelve brothers" (Gen. 42:13E/J). But compare ##26, 94, 122, 144.

#158. < (Neg <M> PpPh)...–Ns ...<C> PpPh>

lō'-ʿālēnū tᵉlunnōtēkem kī ʿal-yahwe, "your complaints are not against us, but against YHWH" (Exod. 16:8P).

#159. <Ni...–IfPh ...<M> PpPh>

ṭōb tittī 'ōtāh lāk mittittī 'ōtāh lᵉ'īš 'aḥēr, "my giving her to you is better than my giving her to another" (Gen. 29:19L). Compare Jon. 4:3, 8.

##160-161. Independent declarative verbless clauses with core <P...–S ...P> plus margins

#160. Voc + <Ni...–Pr ...<Ct> Ns>

rᵉ'ūbēn bᵉkōrī 'attā kōḥī, "Reuben, you are the firstborn of my strength" (Gen. 49:3L). Compare Jer. 31:9.

#161. Md + <Ni...-Pr ...<M> PpPh>

kōl yᵉmē nizrō qādōš hū' lᵉyahwe, "all his vow period he is holy for YHWH" (Num. 6:8P). Other examples: Gen. 42:21E (with this compare Jos. 2:17); Exod. 31:17P.

##162-168. Independent declarative verbless clauses with core <SSus,P–SRes> and no margins

#162. <NSus, (N <Ct> N <Ct> Np)–Pr>

kullām 'ănāšim rā'šē bᵉnē-yiśrā'ēl hēmmā, "all [read enclitic *mem*] the men, heads of the Israelites are they" (Num. 13:3P).

#163. <NSus, Ni–Pr>

zōbō ṭāmē' hū', "his discharge is unclean" (Lev. 15:2P). Another example: Lev. 13:15P.

#164. <NSus, (Ni <M> PpPh)–Pr>

'iš rō'š lᵉbēt-'ăbōtāw hū', "each man is head of his ancestral family" (Num. 1:4P). Similarly Num. 13:32P. Compare Jos. 22:14.

#165. <NSus, (N <Ct> [Ni <A> Ni])–Pr>

kullānū bᵉnē 'iš-'eḥād naḥnū, "all of us, sons of the same man are we" (Gen. 42:11J). Another example: Num. 32:3-4J.

#166. <NSus, Num–Pr>

ḥălōm 'eḥād hū', "the dream is one" (Gen. 41:26E). Other examples: Gen. 40:12E, 18E; 41:25E, 26E.

#167. <NSus, PpPh–Pr>

'ereṣ miṣrayim lᵉpāneykā hī', "the land of Egypt is before you" (Gen. 47:6P).

#168. <NSus, Ni–Ns>

haṣṣūr tāmīm po'ŏlō, "the rock, his work is perfect" (Deut. 32:4). Another example: Gen. 49:20L.

##169-170. Independent declarative verbless clauses with core <SSus,P–SRes> plus margins

#169. Exc + <NSus, (N <Ct> Nd)–Pr>

'ak bᵉ'āśōr laḥōdeš hašššᵉbī'ī hazze yōm hakkippūrīm hū', "yes, the tenth day of this seventh month is the day of atonement" (Lev. 23:27H).

#170. Md + <PpPh,Adv–Pr>

gam-'attā kᵉdibrēkem ken-hū', "now also, like your words, so it is" (Gen. 44:10J). Compare Jos. 2:21; I Sam. 25:25.

##171-174. Independent declarative verbless clauses with core <SSus,P–SRes ...P>

#171. <NSus, Ni...–Pr ...<M> PpPh>
hā'ănāšim hā'ēlle šᵉlēmim hēm 'ittānū, "these men are friendly with us" (Gen. 34:21E). Other examples: Gen. 30:33J; Lev. 11:12P, 20P.

#172. <NSus, (N <Ct> Ni)...–Pr ...<M> PpPh>
kol-ḥērem qōdeš-qodāšim hū' lᵉyahwe, "every devoted thing is most holy for YHWH" (Lev. 27:28P).

#173. <NSus, [(N <Ct> Ni) <M> PpPh...]–Pr ...<C> PpPh>
kol-qorbānām. . . qōdeš qodāšim lᵉkā hū' ūlᵉbāneykā, "all their offering . . . is most holy for you and for your sons" (Num. 18:9P). Compare #149.

#174. <NSus, Ni...–Nd ...<M> Adv>
hā'āreṣ 'ăšer 'ābārnū bāh lātūr 'ōtāh ṭōbā hā'āreṣ mᵉ'ōd mᵉ'ōd, "the land which we passed through to spy out—the land is very very good" (Num. 14:7P).

##175-243. Coordinate declarative verbless clauses with core <S–P> and no margins

#175. *w*– + <Pr–(N <Ct>Np) >
wᵉ'ēlle tōlᵉdōt teraḥ, "and these are the descendants of Terah" (Gen. 11:27P). Other examples: Gen. 25:12P, 19P; 36:1P; Deut. 33:17, 17 but here *hm* is probably "behold!" as in Ugaritic. Similarly Gen. 14: 13P.

#176. *w*– + <Pr–Nd>
wᵉhū' haṣṣā'ir, "and he is the younger" (Gen. 48:14J). Another example: Exod. 9:27J. Compare Judg. 6:15.

#177. *w*– + <Pr–(Nd <A> Nom) >
wᵉze haddābār 'ăšer ta'ăśe lāhem lᵉqaddēš 'ōtām lᵉkahēn li, "and this is the thing that you will do to them to sanctify them to act as priests for me" (Exod. 29:1P). Other examples: Gen. 36:31P; Exod. 21:1C; Deut. 4:44; 6:1; 33:1.

#178. *w*– + <Pr–(N <Ct> Nd) >
wᵉze ša'ar haššāmāyim, "and this is the gate of heaven" (Gen. 28: 17E). Other examples: Lev. 6:7P; 7:1P; Num. 6:13P; Deut. 15:2.

#179. *w*– + <Pr–[(N <Ct> Nd) <A> Nom]>
wᵉze dᵉbar hārōṣēḥ 'ăšer yānūs šāmmā, "and this is the rule for the manslayer who flees there" (Deut. 19:4). Another example: Lev. 7:11P.

#180. w– + <Pr–Nom>
w^eze '$\bar{a}\check{s}er$ ta'$\check{a}\check{s}e$ '$\bar{o}t\bar{a}h$, "and this is what you will make it" (Gen. 6:15P). Another example: Gen. 49:28L.

#181. w– + <Pr–Ns>
w^eze-$piry\bar{a}h$, "and this is its fruit" (Num. 13:27J). Another example: Gen. 36:19P.

#182. w– + <Pr–(Ns <A> Nom) >
$w^eh\bar{e}m$ '$amm^ek\bar{a}$ $w^enah\check{a}l\bar{a}tek\bar{a}$ '$\check{a}\check{s}er$ $h\bar{o}\check{s}\bar{e}$'$t\bar{a}$ $b^ek\bar{o}h\check{a}k\bar{a}$ $hagg\bar{a}d\bar{o}l$ $\bar{u}bizr\bar{o}$'$\check{a}k\bar{a}$ $hann^et\bar{u}y\bar{a}$, "and they are your people and your heritage which you brought out with your great strength and with your extended right arm" (Deut. 9:29). Another example: Deut. 10:21.

#183. w– + <Pr–(Ns <M> PpPh) >
w^eze $zikr\bar{\imath}$ $l^ed\bar{o}r$ $d\bar{o}r$, "and this is my memorial for many generations" (Exod. 3:15E). Another example: Num. 33:2P.

#184. w– + <Pr–(N <Ct> Ns) >
w^e'$\bar{e}lle$ $b^et\bar{u}l\bar{e}$ $bitt\bar{\imath}$, "and these are my daughter's virginity tokens" (Deut. 22:17).

#185. w– + <Pr–PtiPh>
$w^eh\bar{u}$' $y\bar{o}\check{s}\bar{e}b$ $bisd\bar{o}m$, "and he is residing in Sodom" (Gen. 14:12P). Other examples: Gen. 14:13P, 18P; 15:2J; 18:1L, 8L; 24:62J; 32:32L; 34:19J; Num. 22:5J, 22J; 25:6L; 33:40P. Compare Judg. 4:2.

#186. w– + <Pr–(Neg <M> PtiPh) >
$w^eh\bar{u}$' $l\bar{o}$'-$\acute{s}\bar{o}n\bar{e}$' $l\bar{o}$ $mitt^em\bar{o}l$ $\check{s}il\check{s}\bar{o}m$, "and he does not hate him previously" (Deut. 4:42; 19:4). Another example: Num. 35:23P.

#187. w– + <Pr–Ni>
$w^eh\bar{u}$' $t\bar{a}m\bar{e}$', "and he is unclean" (Lev. 5:2P). Other examples: Gen. 18:27J; 19:20J; 25:29L; 27:11J; Lev. 5:1P; 13:21P, 26P, 28P; 19:20H; 22:4H; Deut. 25:18. Similarly Gen. 37:2P; compare Judg. 13:18; Ezek. 33:24.

#188. w– + <Pr–(N <Ct> Ni) >
$w^eh\bar{\imath}$' b^e'$\bar{u}lat$-$b\bar{a}$'al, "and she is married to a husband" (Gen. 20:3E). Other examples: Gen. 34:30L; Exod. 6:12P. Similarly Lev. 24:10H. Compare I Sam. 1:10.

#189. w– + <Pr–PpPh>
$w^eh\bar{u}$' '$ah\check{a}r\bar{a}yw$, "and it is behind him" (Gen. 18:10J). Other examples: Gen. 10:10J; Exod. 16:31L; Lev. 26:34H; Num. 11:26J; 18: 2P; 24:24J; Deut. 33:7. Compare I Sam. 9:22.

#190. $w-$ + <Np–Pti) >

ūpar'ō ḥōlēm, "and Pharaoh is dreaming" (Gen. 41:1E). Other examples: Gen. 18:10J; 19:1L; 23:10P; 25:29J; 27:5J; 29:9J; 30:36L; Exod. 13:21J; 14:27J; Num. 24:18J; 33:4P.

#191. $w-$ + <Np–Ni>

wᵉrāḥēl 'ăqārā, "and Rachel is barren" (Gen. 29:31J). Other examples: Gen. 18:11J; 25:27J/E. Similarly Gen. 13:2L; 24:1E; Num. 22:4J. Compare Judg. 13:2.

#192. $w-$ + <Np–Num>

wᵉnōḥ ben-šēš mē'ōt šānā, "and Noah is six hundred years old" (Gen. 7:6P).

#193. $w-$ + <Np–PpPh>

wᵉyahwe 'ittānū, "and YHWH is with us" (Num. 14:9P). Other examples: Gen. 13:1J; Exod. 19:24J.

#194. $w-$ + < (N <Ct> Np) –Np>

wa'ăḥōt lōṭān timnā', "and Lotan's sister is Timna" (Gen. 36:22P). Other examples: Gen. 4:22L; 10:3P, 4P, 6P, 7P, 7P, 23P; 25:4L; 35:25P, 26P; 46:9P, 10P, 11P, 12P, 13P, 14P, 16P, 17P, 17P, 21P, 23P, 24P; Exod. 6:15P, 18P, 19P, 21P, 22P, 24P; Num. 26:8P, 9P. Similarly Num. 3:19P, 20P.

#195. $w-$ + < (N <Ct> Np) – (N <Ct> Nd) >

ūpᵉquddat 'el'āzār ben-'ahărōn hakkōhēn šemen hammā'ōr ūqᵉtōret hassammīm..., "and the duty of Eleazar ben-Aaron the priest is the lamp oil and the fragrant incense . . ." (Num. 4:16P).

#196. $w-$ + < (N <Ct> Np) –PtiPh>

wᵉrūḥ 'ĕlōhīm mᵉraḥepet 'al-pᵉnē-hammāyim, "and the spirit of God sweeping over the surface of the waters" (Gen. 1:2P). Another example: Exod. 14:8P.

#197. $w-$ + < (N <Ct> Np) –Ni>

wīdē mōše kᵉbēdīm, "and Moses' hands are heavy" (Exod. 17:12J). Other examples: Gen. 13:13L; 29:17L. Compare Jer. 9:25.

#198. $w-$ + < (N <Ct> Np) –Num>

ūbᵉnē yōsēp 'ăšer-yullad-lō bᵉmiṣrayim nepeš šᵉnayim, "and the sons of Joseph that were born to him in Egypt are two persons" (Gen. 46:27P).

#199. $w-$ + < (N <Ct> Np) –PpPh>

wᵉkōs par'ō bᵉyādī, "and Pharaoh's cup is in my hand" (Gen. 40: 11E). Other examples: Num. 17:21P; 23:17E.

#200. *w–* + < (N <Ct> N <Ct> Np) –Np>

wᵉšēm bat-ʾāšēr šārāḥ, "and the name of Asher's daughter is Sarah" (Num. 26:46P). Other examples: Gen. 11:29J; Num. 25:14L; 26:33P, 59P.

#201. *w–* + < (N <Ct> N <Ct> Np) –Nd> plus modifiers
Examples: Num. 3:25P, 36P.

#202. *w–* + < (N <Ct> N <Ct> Np) –PtiPh>

waʾărōn bᵉrīt-yahwe nōsēʿ lipnēhem derek šᵉlōšet yāmīm lātūr lāhem mᵉnūḥā, "and YHWH's covenant ark travels before them a three-day journey to find a campground for them" (Num. 10:33J).

#203. *w–* + <N <Ct> N <Ct> Np) –Num>

ūšᵉnē ḥayyē lēwī šebaʿ ūšᵉlōšīm ūmᵉʾat šānā, "and Levi's life-span is one hundred thirty-seven years" (Exod. 6:16P). Other examples: Exod. 6:18P, 20P; 12:40P. Similarly Num. 4:38-39P, 42-43P.

#204. *w–* + < (N <Ct> N <Ct> Np) –PpPh>

ūmarʾē kᵉbōd yahwe kᵉʾēš ʾōkelet bᵉrōʾš hāhār lᵉʿēnē bᵉnē yiśrāʾēl, "and the appearance of YHWH's glory was like devouring fire on the top of the mountain in the sight of the Israelites" (Exod. 24:17P).

#205. *w–* + < (Ptd <M> PpPh) –Np>

wᵉhaḥōnīm lipnē hammiškān qēdmā lipnē ʾōhel mōʿēd mizrāḥā mōše wᵉʾ ahărōn ūbānāyw, "and the ones camping in front of the meeting tent toward the east are Moses and Aaron and his sons" (Num. 3:38P).

#206. *w–* + < (Ptd <M> PpPh) –(N <Ct> Np) >

wᵉhaḥōnīm ʿālāyw maṭṭē šimʿōn, "and the ones camping beside it are the tribe of Simeon" (Num. 2:12P). Other examples: Num. 2:3P, 5P, 27P.

#207. *w–* + <Nd–(N <Ct> Np) >

wᵉhayyādayim yᵉdē ʿēśāw, "and the hands are Esau's hands" (Gen. 27:22J).

#208. *w–* + <Nd–Ns>

wᵉhabbānīm bānay wᵉhaṣṣōʾn ṣōʾnī, "and the sons are my sons and the flock is my flock" (Gen. 31:43E).

#209. *w–* + <Nd–PtiPh>

wᵉhāhār bōʿēr bāʾēš, "and the mountain is burning with fire" (Deut. 4:11; 5:20; 9:15). Other examples: Gen. 24:21J; 33:13J; 40:17E; Exod. 5:13J; Num. 13:29J, 29J; 14:25J; Deut. 22:6. Similarly Exod. 26:28P.

#210. w- + <Nd–Ni>

w^ehabbōr rēq, "and the pit is empty" (Gen. 37:24E). Other examples: Gen. 24:16J; 43:1J; Exod. 9:31J; 11:3E; Num. 12:3E; 13:28J. Similarly Exod. 28:18P, 19P, 20P; 38:17P; 39:11P, 12P, 13P. With superlative kī Gen. 49:15L.

#211. w- + <Nd–(N <Ct> Ni)>

w^ehā'ănāšīm rō'ē ṣō'n, "and the men are shepherds" (Gen. 46:32J). Other examples: Num. 13:20J; Deut. 11:11 f.

#212. w- + <Nd–Num>

w^ehabbāqār šiššā $ū š^e$lōšīm 'ālep, "and the cattle are 36,000" (Num. 31:38P). Similarly Deut. 2:14.

#213. w- + <Nd–PpPh>

w^ehā'īr battāwek, "and the city is in the middle" (Num. 35:5P). Other examples: Gen. 12:8L; Deut. 29:28. Similarly Lev. 2:3P, 10P.

#214. w- + < (N <Ct> Nd)–Np>

w^ešēm haššēnīt pū'ā, "and the name of the second is Pua" (Exod. 1:15E). Other examples (all with N=šēm): Gen. 2:13J, 14J; 4:19L; 29:16L; Exod. 18:4J; Num. 11:26J; 25:15L. Similarly Num. 3:32P.

#215. w- + < (N <Ct> Nd)–PtiPh>

w^ekol-hā'ām niṣṣāb 'āleykā min-bōqer 'ad-'āreb, "and all the people are standing beside you from morning to evening" (Exod. 18:14J). Other examples: Gen. 24:13J; Exod. 20:18E.

#216. w- + < (N <Ct> Nd)–Ni>

ūba'al haššōr nāqī, "and the owner of the ox is innocent" (Exod. 21:28C). Another example: Gen. 2:12J. Similarly (with PpPh modifying S or P): Exod. 20:10E (=Deut. 5:14); Exod. 27:19P; 38:20P; Lev. 13:3P.

#217. w- + < (N <Ct> Nd)–(N <Ct> Ni)>

w^e'ēmeq haśśiddīm be'ěrōt be'ērōt ḥēmār, "and the valley of the Siddim is all bitumen pits" (Gen. 14:10P). Other examples: Exod. 38:18P; Num. 13:32P.

#218. w- + < (N <Ct> Nd)–Num>

$ūn^e$ḥōšet $hatt^e$nūpā šib'īm kikkār w^e'alpayim w^e'arba'-mē'ōt šāqel, "and the donated bronze is 70 talents and 2400 shekels" (Exod. 38: 29P). Other examples: Exod. 27:12P, 13P; 38:25P; Num. 35:4P.

#219. w- + < (N <Ct> Nd)–PpPh>

ūmaṭṭē hā'ělōhīm b^eyādī, "and the rod of God is in my hand"

73

(Exod. 17:9J). Other examples: Gen. 47:18J; Exod. 32:15E; Num. 31:6P; Deut. 10:3. Similarly Exod. 39:23P; Deut. 9:15.

#220. w– + <Ns–Np>
ūšᵉmāh hāgār, "and her name is Hagar" (Gen. 16:1J). Other examples, all with šēm: Gen. 22:24J; 24:29J; 25:1L; 38:1L, 2L, 6L; Exod. 6:3P. Similarly Exod. 33:11E. Compare Judg. 13:2; Isa. 54:5; Ezek. 23:4.

#221. w– + <Ns–Nd>
ūmišmartām hā'ārōn wᵉhaššulḥān wᵉhammᵉnōrā. . . , "and their responsibility is the ark and the table and the lampstand . . ." (Num. 3:31P). Compare I Sam. 9:21, coordinated with a question.

#222. w– + <Ns–Pti>
wᵉ'ēneykā rā'ōt, "and your eyes are seeing" (Deut. 28:32). Other examples, with Pti modified: Gen. 25:26J; 28:12E; 44:30J; Exod. 2: 5L; Num. 14:14J; 22:23J, 31J.

#223. w– + <Ns–Ni>
wᵉ'ōyᵉbēnū pᵉlīlīm, "and our enemies are judges" (Deut. 32:31). Other examples, in which Ni is the material out of which Ns is made: Exod. 25:38P; 26:21P; 27:10P, 11P, 17P, 18P; 36:26P, 30P, 38P; 38:10P, 19P. Similarly Gen. 18:12J; 18:20J (with superlative kī; compare Gen. 49:15L). Compare Judg. 13:2.

#224. w– + <Ns–(Ni <M> PpPh) >
ūmar'ehā 'āmōq min-hā'ōr, "and its appearance is deeper than the skin" (Lev. 13:25P). Other examples: Gen. 41:21E; Num. 8:8P.

#225. w– + < (Ns <C> Ns) –[(N <Ct> N <Ct> Ni) <M> PpPh]>
ūminḥātām wᵉniskēhem 'iššē rēḥ-nīḥōḥ lᵉyahwe, "and their cereal offering and their libations are a fire offering of pleasing odor for YHWH" (Lev. 23:18H).

#226. w– + <Ns–Num>
wᵉ'ammūdāyw 'eśrīm, "and their pillars are twenty" (Exod. 27:10P, 11P). Other examples: Exod. 27:12P, 14P, 15P, 16P; 38:14P, 15P, 19P; Lev. 23:13H, 13H; Num. 2:4P, 6P, 8P, 11P, 13P, 15P, 19P, 21P, 23P, 26P, 28P, 30P; 7:13-17P. Similarly Num. 3:34P; 31:38P, 39P, 40P.

#227. w– + <Ns–Adv>
ūpᵉnēhem 'āḥorannīt, "and their faces are backwards" (Gen. 9:23L).

#228. w– + <Ns–PpPh>
wᵉṭum'ātō 'ālāyw, "and his uncleanness is on him" (Lev. 7:20P;

22:3H). Other examples: Gen. 6:18P; 7:7J; 8:18P; 11:4L; 19:30L; 24:15J, 45J; Exod. 16:31J; 18:6E; 25:20P; 37:9P; Num. 11:7J; 15:24P; 22:22J; 24:7J.

#229. *w*– + < (N <Ct> Ns) –Np>
w^ešēm 'āḥīw yūbāl, "and his brother's name is Yubal" (Gen. 4:21J).
Other examples, all with *šēm:* Gen. 10:25J; 36:32P, 35P, 39P, 39P; Lev. 24:11H.

#230. *w*– + < (N <Ct> Ns) –Ni>
w^eṣippūy rā'šēhem kāsep, "and the overlay of their capitals is silver" (Exod. 38:17P). Another example: Exod. 38:19P. Compare Jos. 10:2.

#231. *w*– + < (N <Ct> N <Ct> Ns) –PpPh>
w^ekol-ṭūb 'ădōnāyw b^eyādō, "and all his master's property is in his hand" (Gen. 24:10J).

#232. *w*– + < (Ni <M> PpPh) –Np>
w^enāśī' libnē y^ehūdā naḥšōn ben-'ammīnādāb, "and prince for the sons of Judah is Nahshon ben-Amminadab" (Num. 2:3P). The chapter contains twelve such clauses, all P.

#233. *w*– + <Ni–PtiPh>
w^e'ēš mitlaqqaḥat b^etōk habbārād, "and fire is flashing in the midst of the hail" (Exod. 9:24J).

#234. *w*– + <Ni–Num>
w^eqōmā ḥāmēš 'ammōt, "and height five cubits" (Exod. 27:18P). Other examples: Exod. 27:18P; Num. 31:39P, 44P, 45P. Similarly Exod. 38:18P.

#235. *w*– + <Ni–PpPh>
w^eḥōšek 'al-p^enē-t^ehōm, "and darkness is on the surface of the deep" (Gen. 1:2P). Other examples: Exod. 14:7J; 25:35P, 35P, 35P; 37:21P, 21P, 21P; Num. 22:7J. Compare I Sam. 25:25. Similarly, with negation: Num. 23:23E; compare Jos. 17:17; Jer. 10:14.

#236. *w*– + <[(N <Ct> N <Ct> Ni) <M> PpPh]–Np>
ūn^eśī' bēt-'āb laggēršunnī 'elyāsāp ben-lā'ēl, "and father-house prince for the Gershunnites is Elyasaph ben-Lael" (Num. 3:24P). Other examples: Num. 3:30P, 35P.

#237. *w*– + < (N <Ct> Ni) –Num>
w^enepeš 'ādām šiššā 'āśār 'ālep, "and human beings are sixteen thousand" (Num. 31:40P). Another example: Num. 31:46P.

#238. w- + < (N <Ct> Ni) –PpPh>

ūterū'at melek bō, "and a royal shout is in it" (Num. 23:21E). Another example: Gen. 16:12J. Similarly: Exod. 13:12L; 28:33P; Lev. 13:10P.

#239. w- + <Num–PtiPh>

wešiššā qānīm yōṣe'īm miṣṣiddeyhā, "and six branches are going out of its sides" (Exod. 25:32P; 37:18P).

#240. w- + <Num–PpPh>

we'arba'-mē'ōt 'īš 'immō, "and four hundred men are with him" (Gen. 32:7J). Other examples: Gen. 11:6L; Exod. 25:12P, 32P, 33P; 26:21P; 29:40P; 36:26P.

#241. w- + <PpPh–Ni>

ūbayyōm haššebī'ī šabbāt, "and on the seventh day is sabbath" (Exod. 16:26J). Other examples: Lev. 23:39H; Num. 28:17P. Similarly: Exod. 13:6L; Num. 28:16P; Deut. 16:8.

#242. w- + <PpPh–(N <Ct> Ni) >

ūbayyōm hārī'šōn miqrā'-qōdeš, "and on the first day is a holy meeting" (Exod. 12:16P). Other examples: Exod. 31:15P; Lev. 23:3H, 6H.

#243. w- + <PpPh–PpPh>

wetahat raglāyw kema'áśē libnat hassappīr ūke'eṣem haššāmayim lāṭohar, "and under his feet is like a pavement of sapphire, like the sky itself in clarity" (Exod. 24:10L). Other examples: Num. 21:16E; Deut. 9:10.

#244-254. Coordinate declarative verbless clauses with core <S–P> plus margins

#244. w- + <Pr–(N <Ct> Np) > + PpPh

we'elle tōledōt 'ēśāw 'ăbī 'ĕdōm behar śē'īr, "and these are the descendants of Esau, the ancestor of Edom, in the mountain country of Seir" (Gen. 36:9P). Another example: Num. 3:1P.

#245. w- + <Pr–[PpPh]–Nd>

weze-llekā hā'ōt kī 'ānōkī šelaḥtīkā, "and this is the sign for you that I have sent you" (Exod. 3:12E).

#246. w- + <Pr–[PpPh]–(N <Ct> Ns) >

weze-llekā terūmat mattānām, "and this is their gift offering for you" (Num. 18:11P).

#247. w- + <Np–(N <Ct> Num) > + IfPh

ūmōše ben–mē'ā we'eśrīm šānā bemōtō, "and Moses was one hundred twenty years old when he died" (Deut. 34:7P). Other examples: Gen. 12:4P; 16:16P; 17:24P, 25P; 21:5P; 25:26P; 41:46P; Exod. 7:7P; Num. 33:39P. Compare #137.

#248. w- + < (N <Ct> Np) –PpPh> + Adv + IfPh
wa‘ănan yahwe ‘ălēhem yōmām bᵉnos‘ām min-hammaḥăne, "and the cloud of YHWH is over them by day when they set out from the camp" (Num. 10:34J).

#249. w- + < (Nd <C> Nd) –[Adv]–PtiPh>
wᵉhakkᵉna‘ănī wᵉhappᵉrizzī ’āz yōšēb bā’āreṣ, "and the Canaanite and the Perizzite then dwelt in the land" (Gen. 13:7J).

#250. w- + <Nd–[PpPh]–(Ni <M> PpPh) >
wᵉhammayim lāhem ḥōmā mīmīnām ūmiśśᵉmō’lām, "and for them the water is a wall on their right and on their left" (Exod. 14:22E, 29E).

#251. w- + <Nd–[Adv]–PpPh>
wᵉhaqqāṭōn hayyōm ’et-’ābīnū bᵉ’ereṣ kᵉnā‘an, "and the younger is at present with our father in the land of Canaan" (Gen. 42:32E).

#252. w- + < (N <Ct> N <Ct> Nd) –PpPh> + IfPh
ūšᵉnē luḥōt hā’ēdūt bᵉyad-mōše bᵉridtō min hāhār, "and the two tablets of testimony were in Moses' hand when he came down from the mountain" (Exod. 34:29P).

#253. w- + Adv + <Ns–Ni>
wᵉ‘attā napšēnū yᵉbēšā, "and now our throats are parched" (Num. 11:6J).

#254. w- + < (N <Ct> N <Ct> N <Ct> Ns) – (Adv <M> Ni) >
+ Adv
wᵉkol-yēṣer maḥšᵉbōt libbō raq ra‘ kol hayyōm, "and every imagination of the thoughts of his heart is only evil all the time" (Gen. 6:5J).

#255-269. Coordinate declarative verbless clauses with core <S... –P ...S> and no margins

#255. w- + <Pr...– (N <Ct> Np) ...List>
wᵉ’ēlle bᵉnē rᵉ‘ū’ēl naḥat wāzeraḥ šammā ūmizzā, "and these are Reuel's sons—Nahath and Zerah, Shamma and Mizza" (Gen. 36:13P). Other examples: Gen. 10:1P; 36:17P, 18P, 23P, 24P, 25P, 26P; 46:8-9P; Exod. 1:1-4P; Num. 3:2P. Similarly: Gen. 25:13P; 36:40-43P; Exod. 6:16P; Num. 3:18P; 26:36P.

#256. w– + <Pr...–(N <Ct> N <Ct> Np) ...Num>

weʾēlle šenē ḥayyē yišmāʿ ʾēl meʾat šānā ūšelōšīm šānā wešebaʿ šānīm, "and these are the years of the life of Ishmael—one hundred thirty-seven years" (Gen. 25:17P). Another example: Gen. 25:7P.

#257. w– + <Pr...–(Nd <A> Nom) ...Ni>

wezōʾt hatterūmā ʾăšer tiqḥū mēʾittām zāhāb wākesep ūneḥōšet, "and this is the offering that you shall receive from them—gold and silver and bronze" (Exod. 25:3P). Another example: Exod. 28:4P.

#258. w– + <Pr...–(N <Ct> Nd) ...(PpPh <M> Np) >

weʾēlle šemōt hāʾănāšīm lemaṭṭē yehūdā kālēb ben-yepunne ūlemaṭṭē benē šimʿōn šemūʾēl ben-ʿammihūd. . . , "and these are the names of the men—for the tribe of Judah, Caleb ben-Jephunneh; for the tribe of the sons of Simeon, Shemuel ben-Ammihud . . ." (Num. 34:19-28P). Other examples: Num. 1:5-15P; Num. 26:57P.

#259. w– + <Pr...–(N <Ct> Nd) ...Ni>

weze maʿăśē hammenōrā miqšā zāhāb, "and this is the workmanship of the lampstand—hammered gold" (Num. 8:4P).

#260. w– <Pr...–Nom ...Ni>

weze ʾăšer taʿăśe ʿal-hammizbēḥ kebāśīm benē šānā šenayim layyōm tāmīd, "and this is what you will offer upon the altar—one-year-old lambs, two a day perpetually" (Exod. 29:38P). Another example: Deut. 14:12-18.

#261. w– + <Pr...–Ns ...Np>

weʾēlle šemōtām lemaṭṭē reʾūbēn šammūʿ ben-zakkūr. . . , "and these are their names—for the tribe of Reuben, Shammua ben-Zakkur . . ." (Num. 13:4-15P).

#262. w– + <Pr...–(Ns <M> PpPh) ...Num>

weʾēlle šemōtām beḥaṣrēhem ūbeṭīrōtām šenēm-ʿāśār neśīʾīm leʾummōtām, "and these are their names by their enclosures and fortifications—twelve princes for their clans" (Gen. 25:16P).

#263. w– + <Pr...–(N <Ct> Ns) ...Np>

weʾēlle šemōt benōtāyw maḥlā nōʿā weḥoglā ūmilkā wetirṣā, "and these are the names of his daughters—Mahlah, Noah and Hoglah and Milkah and Tirzah" (Num. 27:1P). Similarly: Num. 4:31-32P.

#264. w– + <Pr...–PtiPh ...(N <Ct> N <Ct> Nd) >

wehēm meḥuššāqīm kesep kōl ʿammūdē heḥāṣēr, "and these are filleted with silver—all the posts of the court" (Exod. 38:17P).

#265. w– + <Nd...–Ni ...<M> PpPh>

w⁽ᵉ⁾hā’eben g⁽ᵉ⁾dōlā ‘al-pī-habbe’ēr, "and the stone on the well's mouth was large" (Gen. 29:2L).

#266. w– + <N <Ct>...–Num ...Nd>

w⁽ᵉ⁾rōḥab ’arba‘ bā’ammā hay⁽ᵉ⁾rī‘ā hā’eḥāt, "and the breadth of each curtain is four cubits" (Exod. 26:2P). Other examples: Exod. 26:8P; 36:9P.

#267. w– + < (N <Ct> Nd)...–PpPh ...<C> (N <Ct> NdPh) >

w⁽ᵉ⁾ēṣ haḥayyīm b⁽ᵉ⁾tōk haggān w⁽ᵉ⁾ēṣ hadda‘at ṭōb wārā‘, "and the tree of life and the tree of the knowledge of good and evil are in the midst of the garden" (Gen. 2:9L).

#268. w– + <Ns...–PtiPh ...<A> PtiPh>

ūg⁽ᵉ⁾mallēhem nōś⁽ᵉ⁾’īm n⁽ᵉ⁾kō’t ūṣ⁽ᵉ⁾rī wālōṭ hōl⁽ᵉ⁾kīm l⁽ᵉ⁾hōrīd miṣrāymā, "and their camels are carrying gum, balm, and myrrh, going right down to Egypt" (Gen. 37:25J).

#269. w– + <Ns...–PpPh ...<C> (Ns <A> Nom) >

ūn⁽ᵉ⁾dāreyhā ‘āleyhā ’ō mibṭā’ ś⁽ᵉ⁾pāteyhā ’ǎšer ’āś⁽ᵉ⁾rā ‘al-napšāh, "and her vows or foolish utterances by which she bound herself are against her" (Num. 30:7P).

#270. Coordinate declarative verbless clause with core <S...–P ... S> plus margin

#270. w– + <Pr...[PpPh]–(Nd <M> PpPh) ...Nd>

w⁽ᵉ⁾ze lākem haṭṭāmē’ baššereṣ haššōrēṣ ‘al-hā’āreṣ hahōled w⁽ᵉ⁾hā‘akbār w⁽ᵉ⁾haṣṣāb..., "and for you this is the unclean among the swarming things that swarm upon the earth—the weasel, the mouse, the lizard ..." (Lev. 11:29P).

##271-272. Coordinate declarative verbless clauses with core <P... S–...P> and no margins

#271. w– + <Md <M>... Pr–...PtiPh>

w⁽ᵉ⁾’ēlāyw hū’ nōśē ’et-napšō, "and he is putting his desire on it" (Deut. 24:15). Another example: Num. 14:14J. Similarly: Deut. 29: 13.

#272. w– + <Md <M>... Np–...PtiPh>

wa’ǎšer hū’ ‘ōśe yahwe maṣlīḥ, "and what he is doing YHWH makes successful" (Gen. 39:23J). Other examples: Gen. 39:3J; Deut. 9:4; 18:12.

#273. Coordinate declarative verbless clause with core <P... S–...P> plus margin

#273. *w–* + Cl + <PpPh... Ni–...Pti>
we'im lō' tēṭīb lappetaḥ ḥaṭṭā't rōbēṣ, "and if you do not do well, at the door sin is lying" (Gen. 4:7J).

##274-279. Coordinate declarative verbless clauses with core <SSus,SRes–P>

#274. *w–* + <NSus,PrRes–Np>
wehannāhār hārebī'ī hū' perāt, "and the fourth river is Perath" (Gen. 2:14J). Another example: Gen. 15:2J.

#275. *w–* + <NSus,PrRes–(N <Ct> Np)>
weḥām hū' 'ăbī kena'an, "and Ham is the ancestor of Canaan" (Gen. 9:18J).

#276. *w–* + <NSus,PrRes–(Nd <M> PpPh)>
weyōsēp hū' haššallīṭ 'al-hā'āreṣ, "and Joseph is the vizier over the land" (Gen. 42:6E). Compare I Sam. 17:12.

#277. *w–* + <NSus,PrRes–PtdPh>
weyahwe hū' hahōlēk lepāneykā, "and YHWH, he is the one who walks before you" (Deut. 31:8).

#278. *w–* + <NSus,PrRes–Ns>
wekōl 'ăšer yiqrā'-lō hā'ādām nepeš ḥayyā hū' šemō, "and whatever the man would call an animal, that was its name" (Gen. 2:19J).

#279. *w–* + <NSus,PrRes–Num>
wehā'ăbānīm 'al-šemōt benē yiśrā'ēl hēnnā šetēm 'eśrē 'al-šemōtām, "and the stones corresponding to the names of the sons of Israel are twelve, corresponding to their names" (Exod. 39:14P).

#280. Coordinate declarative verbless clause with core <SSus,P... SRes–...P>

#280. *w–* + <(Nd <A> Nom)Sus, Md <M>... PrRes–...Pti>
wehannepeš 'ăšer-ta'ăśe beyād rāmā min-hā'ezraḥ ūmin-haggēr 'et-yahwe hū' megaddēp, "and the person who acts with a high hand, any native or alien, he insults YHWH" (Num. 15:30P).

##281-299. Coordinate declarative verbless clauses with core <P–S> and no margins

#281. w– + <PtiPh–Pr>

w^egam 'et-haggōy 'ăšer ya'ăbōdū dān 'ānōkī, "and the nation also that they serve I am judging" (Gen. 15:14E).

#282. w– + <Ni–Pr>

ūṭehōrā hī', "and she is clean" (Num. 5:28P).

#283. w– + <[Adv <M> (N <Ct> [Ni <C> Ni])]–Pr>

w^egam zābat ḥālāb ūd^{e}baš hī', "and it is even flowing with milk and honey" (Num. 13:27J).

#284. w– + <Adv–Np>

w^ešām 'ăḥīmān šēšay w^etalmay y^elīdē hā'ănāq, "and Ahiman, Sheshai, and Talmai, descendants of the Anaq, are there" (Num. 13:22J). Compare ##294, 297; contrast Num. 14:43.

#285. w– + <PpPh–Np>

ūb^{e}tōkām yahwe, "and YHWH is in the midst of them" (Num. 16: 3P). Other examples: Exod. 38:23P; Num. 10:14P, 15P, 16P, 18P, 19P, 20P, 22P, 23P, 24P, 25P, 26P, 27P. Compare Judg. 4:2, which suggests that 'al in Num 10 is a noun (=šar). See p. 41.

#286. w– + <PpPh–(N <Ct> Np)>

we'ālāyw maṭṭē m^enašše, "and the tribe of Manasseh is beside it" (Num. 2:20P).

#287. w– + <Ni–Nd>

w^erak hallēbāb, "and weak is the heart" (Deut. 20:8), a doubtful example. Compare Koh. 11:7; Dan. 10:1.

#288. w– + <Num–(N <Ct> Nd)>

we'arba' 'ammōt rōḥab hay^{e}rī'ā hā'eḥāt, "and four cubits is the breadth of each curtain" (Exod. 36:15P). Other examples: Exod. 26: 16P; 36:20P.

#289. w– + <(N <Ct> Ni)–Ns>

w^eqarnē re'ēm qarnāyw, "and his horns are the horns of a wild ox" (Deut. 33:17). Another example: Deut. 32:33. Compare Isa. 48:4; Nah. 1:3.

#290. w– + <Num–Ns>

ūš^{e}lōšim 'ammā qōmātāh, "and its height is thirty cubits" (Gen. 6:15P). Other examples: Exod. 25:10P, 10P, 17P, 23P, 23P; 27:1P; 28:16P; 30:2P, 2P; 37:1P, 1P, 6P, 10P, 10P, 25P, 25P; 38:1P, 1P; 39:9P.

#291. w– + <PpPh–Ns>

we'el-'īšēk t^ešūqātēk, "and your desire is to your husband" (Gen. 3: 16L). Other examples: Gen. 4:7J; Num. 32:32J; Deut. 33:25.

#292. w- + <Ni–Ni>

weʾepes ʿāṣūr weʿāzūb, "and bond and free are nothing" (Deut. 32:36).

#293. w- + <Num–Ni>

weʿeśrīm ʾammā ʾōrek, "and length is twenty cubits" (Exod. 38:18P). Other examples: Exod. 27:1P, 14P.

#294. w- + < (Adv <M> PpPh)–Ni>

wešām ʾittānū naʿar ʿibrī ʿebed leśar haṭṭabbāḥīm, "and with us there is a Hebrew lad, slave of the captain of the bodyguard" (Gen. 41:12E).

#295. w- + <PpPh–Ni>

welāh šipḥā miṣrīt, "and she has an Egyptian slave" (Gen. 16:1J). Other examples: Gen. 18:14J; 24:29E; Lev. 13:30P; Num. 32:4J. Compare Num. 28:16P.

#296. w- + <PpPh–(N <Ct> Ni) >

ūmittaḥat zirʿōt ʿōlām, "and eternal arms are underneath" (Deut. 33:27). Another example: Gen. 49:10L.

#297. w- + <Adv–Num>

wešām šetēm ʿeśrē ʿēnōt mayim wešibʿīm temārīm, "and twelve water springs and seventy palm trees are there" (Exod. 15:27L).

#298. w- + <PpPh–Num>

weʿimmō ʾarbaʿ mēʾōt ʾīš, "and four hundred men are with him" (Gen. 33:1J). Other examples: Gen. 29:16J; 40:10E; Exod. 2:16L; 25:34P; 26:20P; 27:11P, 15P, 16P; 37:20P; Num. 33:9P.

#299. w- + <Ni–IfPh>

werab mihyōt qōlōt ʾelōhīm ūbārād, "and the thunder and hail of God is enough" (Exod. 9:28J). Compare #129, which suggests *wrbm*, with enclitic *m*.

##300-303. Coordinate declarative verbless clauses with core <P–S> plus margins

#300. w- + Adv + <Ns–Pr>

wegam-ʾomnā ʾăḥōtī bat-ʾābī hī, "and also indeed she is my sister, my father's daughter" (Gen. 20:12E).

#301. w- + Adv + <Ni–Pr>

weʾūlām ḥay-ʾānī, "and truly I live" (Num. 14:21J). Another example: Deut. 30:11. Compare I Kings 20:28; Jer. 4:22.

#302. *w*– + Cl + <Ni–Pr>

we'im-'ayin mētā 'ānōkī, "and if not, I am dead" (Gen. 30:1E).
Other examples: Lev. 13:41P, 57P; 19:7H; 20:14H, 17H, 21H.

#303. *w*– + Adv + <Np–(N <Ct> Nd) > + Adv

we'ūlām lūz šēm-hā'īr lārī'šōnā, "but actually the name of the city
was Luz previously" (Gen. 28:19J).

##304-308. Coordinate declarative verbless clauses with core <P ...–S ...P> and no margins

#304. *w*– + < (Neg <M> PpPh)...–Pr ...IfPh>

welō'-mē'ēber layyām hī' lē'mōr, "and it is not across the sea, saying"
(Deut. 30:13).

#305. *w*– + <Pti...–Np ...IfPh>

ūmemahēr hā'ělōhīm la'ăśōtō, "and God is hurrying to do it" (Gen.
41:32E).

#306. *w*– + <Ni...–Nd ...IfPh>

wenehmād hā'ēṣ lehaśkīl, "and the tree is desirable for being wise"
(Gen. 3:6L).

#307. *w*– + <Num...–Ns ...PpPh>

we'arba' 'ammōt roḥbāh be'ammat-'īš, "and its width is four cubits
by the secular cubit" (Deut. 3:11).

#308. *w*– + <Ni...–Ni ...<M> PpPh>

ūleben-šinnayim mēhālāb, "and teeth are whiter than milk" (Gen.
49:12L).

#309. Coordinate declarative verbless clause with core <P...–S ...P> plus margin

#309. *w*– + Cl + < (Ni <A> Pti...)–Pr ...<M> PpPh>

*wekī-yihye baqqārahat 'ō baggabbahat nega' lābān 'ădamdām ṣāra'at
pōrahat hī' beqārahtō 'ō begabbahtō*, "and if there is on the crown or
on the forehead a red-white lesion, it is leprosy breaking out on his
crown or on his forehead" (Lev. 13:42P).

##310-315. Coordinate declarative verbless clauses with core <SSus,P–SRes> and no margins

#310. *w*– + <NdSus, (N <Ct> Np)–PrRes>

wehallūḥōt ma'ăśē 'ělōhīm hēmmā, "and the tablets, they are the
work of God" (Exod. 32:16E).

#311. *w–* + <NdSus, (N <Ct> Nd) –PrRes>

wᵉhāʿōmer ʿăśīrīt hāʾēpā hūʾ, "and the omer is one-tenth of the ephah" (Exod. 16:36L).

#312. *w–* + <NSus,Ni–PrRes>

wᵉkol-haśśereṣ haśśōrēṣ ʿal-hāʾāreṣ śeqeṣ hūʾ, "and every swarming thing that swarms on the earth is an abomination" (Lev. 11:41P). Another example: Num. 19:15P.

#313. *w–* + < (Nd <A> Nom) Sus, (N <Ct> Ni) –PrRes>

wᵉhāʾāreṣ ʾăśer hikkā yahwe lipnē ʿădat yiśrāʾēl ʾereṣ miqne hīʾ, "and the land which YHWH smote before the community of Israel is livestock land" (Num. 32:4J).

#314. *w–* + <NumdSus,Numi–PrRes>

wᵉśebaʿ haśśibbŏlīm haṭṭōbōt śebaʿ śānīm hēnnā, "and the seven good ears are seven years" (Gen. 41:26E). Another example: Gen. 41: 27E.

#315. *w–* + <NdSus,PpPh–PrRes>

wᵉhammān kizraʿ-gad hūʾ, "and the manna is like coriander seed" (Num. 11:7E). Similarly: Gen. 31:43E.

##316-317. Coordinate declarative verbless clauses with core <SSus,P–SRes> plus margins

#316. *w–* + < (Pr <A> NdPh) Sus,Ni–PrRes> + Adv

wᵉʾattem haddᵉbēqīm bᵉyahwe ʾĕlōhēkem ḥayyīm kullᵉkem hayyōm, "and you who adhered to YHWH your god, all of you are alive today" (Deut. 4:4).

#317. *w–* + Adv + <NumPhSus,PpPh–PrRes>

wᵉʾattā śᵉnē bāneykā hannōlādīm lᵉkā bᵉʾereṣ miṣrayim ʿad-bōʾī ʾēleykā miṣraymā lī-hēm, "and now, your two sons who were born to you in the land of Egypt before I came to you to Egypt, they are mine" (Gen. 48:5P).

##318-320. Coordinate declarative verbless clauses with core <SSus,P...–SRes ...P> and no margins

#318. *w–* + <NdSus, (N <Ct> Np)...–PrRes ...<A> PtiPh>

wᵉhammiktāb miktab ʾĕlōhīm hūʾ ḥārūt ʿal-hallūḥōt, "and the inscription is an inscription of God, engraved on the tablets" (Exod. 32:16E).

#319. *w–* + <NSus,Ni...–PrRes ...<M> PpPh>

wᵉkōl śereṣ hāʿōp ṭāmēʾ hūʾ lākem, "and all winged insects are unclean for you" (Deut. 14:19). Other examples: Lev. 11:10P, 23P, 26P, 27P.

#320. w– + <NSus,PpPh...–PrRes ...<A> Ni>

$w^ekol-ma'\check{s}ar$ $h\bar{a}'\bar{a}re\d{s}$ $mizzera'$ $h\bar{a}'\bar{a}re\d{s}$ $mipp^er\bar{\imath}$ $h\bar{a}'\bar{e}\d{s}$ l^eyahwe $h\bar{u}'$ $q\bar{o}de\check{s}$ l^eyahwe, "and all the tithe of the land, from the seed of the land and from the fruit of trees, it is YHWH's, holy for YHWH" (Lev. 27:30P). Similarly: Exod. 39:5P. Compare II Sam. 21:2.

#321. Coordinate declarative verbless clause with core <PSus, PRes–S> plus margin

#321.* gm– + Adv + <PpPhSus,AdvRes–Pr>

$gam-'att\bar{a}$ $k^edibr\bar{e}kem$ $k\bar{e}n-h\bar{u}'$, "and now, according to your words, so it is" (Gen. 44:10J). Compare #170.

##322-351. Subordinate declarative verbless clauses with core <S–P> and no margins

#322.* Cj + <Pr–Pr>

$k\bar{\imath}-ze$ $h\bar{u}'$, "for this is he" (I Sam. 16:12). Compare #368.

#323. Cj + <Pr–Np>

$k\bar{\imath}$ $'\check{a}n\bar{\imath}$ $yahwe$, "for I am YHWH" (Exod. 7:5P, 17P; 10:2J; 14:4L; 14:18E). Other examples, in which Np is modified: Exod. 6:7P; 8:18J; 15:26L; 16:12P; 20:5E; 29:46P; 31:13P; Lev. 11:44P, 45P; 20:7H; 21:15H, 23H; 22:16H; 24:22H; 25:17H; 26:1H, 44H; Num. 35:34P; Deut. 5:9; 29:5.

#324. Cj + <Pr–Nd>

$k\bar{\imath}$ ze $habb^ek\bar{o}r$, "for this is the firstborn" (Gen. 48:18J). Another example: Deut. 7:7.

#325. Cj + <Pr–[(N <Ct> Nd) <C> Ns]>

$k\bar{\imath}$ $h\bar{e}m$ $ziqn\bar{e}$ $h\bar{a}'\bar{a}m$ $w^e\check{s}\bar{o}t^er\bar{a}yw$, "that they are the elders of the people and its officers" (Num. 11:16E).

#326. Cj + <Pr–PtdPh>

$k\bar{\imath}$ $h\bar{u}'$ $hann\bar{o}t\bar{e}n$ $l^ek\bar{a}$ $k\bar{o}\d{h}$ $la'\check{a}\acute{s}\bar{o}t$ $\d{h}\bar{a}yil$, "for he is the one who gives you strength to make wealth" (Deut. 8:18). Similarly: Num. 16:11P.

#327. Cj + <Pr–Ns>

$k\bar{\imath}-h\bar{u}'$ $\d{h}ayy\bar{e}kem$, "for it is your life" (Deut. 32:47). Similarly: Exod. 22:26C; Deut. 4:6; 30:20.

#328. Cj + <Pr–(N <Ct> Ns)>

$k\bar{\imath}-h\bar{u}'$ $r\bar{e}'\check{s}\bar{\imath}t$ $'\bar{o}n\bar{o}$, "for he is the first of his strength" (Deut. 21:17).

#329. Cj + <Pr–PtiPh>

kī-'attem bā'im 'el-hā'āreṣ kᵉnāʿan, "when you enter the land of Canaan" (Num. 34:2P). Other examples: Gen. 13:10L; 45:26J; Exod. 5:8J, 17J; 13:15L; 16:29L; Num. 22:34J; 33:51P; 35:10P, 34P; Deut. 4:22; 11:31; 15:11, 15; 18:9; 19:7; 24:18, 22.

#330.* Cj + <Pr–(Ni <M> PpPh)>

wᵉkī hī' gᵉdōlā min-hā'ay, "and that it is bigger than Ay" (Jos. 10:2E). Another example: I Kings 21:2.

#331. Cj + <(Pr <A> Np)–PpPh>

kī-'attā yahwe bᵉqereb hāʿām hazze, "that you, YHWH, are in the midst of this people" (Num. 14:14J).

#332. Cj + <Np–[(N <Ct> Np) <M> PpPh]>

kī 'arnōn gᵉbūl mō'āb bēn mō'āb ūbēn hā'ĕmōrī, "for Arnon is the boundary of Moab between Moab and the Amorite" (Num. 21:13E).

#333. Cj + <Np–Nd>

kī mᵉnašše habbᵉkōr, "for Manasse is the firstborn" (Gen. 48:14E).

#334. Cj + <(Np <A> Ns)–PtdPh>

kī yahwe 'ĕlōhēkem hahōlēk ʿimmākem lᵉhillāḥēm lākem ʿim-'oyᵉbēkem lᵉhōšīʿ 'etkem, "for YHWH your god is the one who walks with you to fight for you with your enemies to rescue you" (Deut. 20:4).

#335. Cj + <Np–PtiPh>

kī yahwe nilḥām lāhem bᵉmiṣrāyim, "for YHWH is fighting for them against Egypt" (Exod. 14:25J). Another example: Deut. 8:7.

#336. Cj + <Np–PpPh>

kī yahwe 'ittō, "that YHWH is with him" (Gen. 39:3J).

#337. Cj + <(N <Ct> Np)–Ns>

kī ḥēleq yahwe ʿammō, "for YHWH's allotment is his people" (Deut. 32:9P).

#338. Cj + <(N <Ct> Np)–PpPh>

kī ḥag-yahwe lānū, "for we have a YHWH festival" (Exod. 10:9J). Another example: Lev. 10:7P.

#339. Cj + <Nd–Ni>

kī-hayᵉlādīm rakkīm, "that the children are frail" (Gen. 33:13J). Another example: Exod. 9:31J. Compare Ezek. 42:13.

#340. Cj + <Nd–PpPh>

kī hammēlīṣ bēnōtām, "for the interpreter is between them" (Gen. 42:23E) . Similarly: Num. 14:43J.

#341.* Cj + < (N <Ct> Nd) –Ni>

kī kol-haggōyīm 'ărēlīm, "for all the nations are uncircumcized" (Jer. 9:25) . Similarly: I Kings 8:64.

#342. Cj + < (N <Ct> Nd) –PpPh>

kī-'ăbōdat haqqōdeš 'ălēhem, "because the holy service is upon them" (Num. 7:9P) .

#343. Cj + <Ns–PtdPh>

kī-pī hammᵉdabbēr 'ălēkem, "that my mouth is what is talking to you" (Gen. 45:12E) . Another example: Deut. 11:7.

#344.* Cj + <Ns-(Ni <M> PpPh) >

kī-napšāh mārā-lāh, "for her soul is bitter for her" (II Kings 4:27) . Similarly: I Sam. 19:4.

#345. Cj + <Ns–PpPh>

'im-bᵉ'ālāyw 'immō, "if its owner is with it" (Exod. 22:14C) . Other examples: Exod. 23:21C; Lev. 22:25H.

#346. Cj + < (N <Ct> Ns) –Ni>

kī kol-dᵉrākāyw mišpāṭ, "for all his ways are right" (Deut. 32:4) .

#347. Cj + < (N <Ct> Ns) –PpPh>

kī nēzer 'ĕlōhāyw 'al-rō'šō, "for his god's dedication is on his head" (Num. 6:7P) . Other examples: Exod. 18:4J; Lev. 21:12H.

#348. Cj + <Ni–PpPh>

kī mūm bō, "for a blemish is in it" (Lev. 21:23H) . Other examples: Gen. 8:9J; 25:28J; Exod. 10:10J; 17:16J; Deut. 3:19. Compare Jos. 3:10.

#349. Cj + < (N <Ct> Ni) –Ni>

'im kol-bᵉhēmā ṭᵉmā'ā, "if any animal is unclean" (Lev. 27:11P) .

#350. Cj + < (N <Ct> Ni) –PpPh>

kī-derek nāšīm lī, "for I have the way of women" (Gen. 31:35E) . Another example: Num. 23:22E; 24:8J. Compare Ezek. 32:27.

#351. Cj + <Num–PpPh>

kī maṭṭe 'eḥad lᵉrō'š bēt 'ăbōtām, "for their family head has one rod" Num. 17:18P) .

##352-355. Subordinate declarative verbless clauses with core <S–P> plus margins

#352. Cj + < (N <Ct> Np) –PpPh> +Adv
kī 'ănan yahwe 'al-hammiškān yōmām, "for YHWH's cloud is over the tabernacle by day" (Exod. 40:38P).

#353. Cj + Adv + <Nd–PpPh>
kī-ze šᵉnātayim hārā'āb bᵉqereb hā'āreṣ, "for now two years the famine is in the midst of the land" (Gen. 45:6E).

#354. Cj + < (N <Ct> Nd) –Np> + Adv
'al-kēn šēm-hā'īr bᵉ'ēr šeba' 'ad hayyōm hazze, "therefore the name of the city is Beer-sheba until this day" (Gen. 26:33J).

#355. Cj + < (N <Ct> N <Ct> Nd) –Ni> + PpPh
kī yēṣer lēb hā'ādām ra' minnᵉ'ūrāyw, "for the tendency of the heart of man is evil from his youth" (Gen. 8:21J).

#356. Subordinate declarative verbless clause with core <S. . .–P . . .S> and no margin

#356. Cj + < (Np <A> Ns) . . .–PpPh . . .<A> NiPh>
kī-yahwe 'ĕlōheykā bᵉqirbekā 'ēl gādōl wᵉnōrā', "for YHWH your god is in your midst, a great and terrifying god" (Deut. 7:21). Another example: Deut. 20:1.

##357-359. Subordinate declarative verbless clauses with core <P. . . S–. . .P> and no margins

#357. Cj + <Md <M>. . . Pr–. . .Pti>
kī 'ōtāh 'attem mᵉbaqᵉšīm, "for you are seeking it" (Exod. 10:11J). Other examples: Gen. 7:4J; Exod. 9:14J; Lev. 3:1P, 7P; 21:6H, 8H; 25:16H; Num. 11:15J; Deut. 24:6.

#358. Cj + <Md <M>. . . Np–. . .Pti>
kī hayyōm yahwe nir'ā 'ălēkem, "for today YHWH is showing himself to you" (Lev. 9:4P). Other examples: Deut. 8:5; 9:5, 6.

#359. Cj + <Md <M>. . . (N <Ct> Ni) –. . .Pti>
kī-šām ḥelqat mᵉḥōqēq sāpūn, "for there a legislator's portion is reserved" (Deut. 33:21).

##360-366. Subordinate declarative verbless clauses with core <SSus,SRes–P> and no margins

#360. Cj + <PrSus,PrRes–Pr>
kī 'ănī 'ănī hū', "that I, I am he" (Deut. 32:39).

#361. Cj + <NSus,PrRes–Nd>

kī yahwe hū' hā'ĕlōhīm, "that YHWH, he is God" (Deut. 4:35, 39). Other examples: Deut. 7:9; 12:23.

#362. Cj + <NSus,PrRes–(N <Ct> Nd)...>

kī yahwe 'ĕlōhēkem hū' 'ĕlōhē hā'ĕlōhīm wa'ădōnē hā'ădōnīm ..., "for YHWH your god is god of gods and lord of lords ..." (Deut. 10: 17).

#363. Cj + <NSus,PrRes–PtdPh>

kī yahwe 'ĕlōheykā hū' hahōlēk 'immāk, "for YHWH your god, he is the one who goes with you" (Deut. 31:6). Other examples: Deut. 3:22; 9:3.

#364. Cj + <NdSus,PrRes–Nom>

kī haddām hū' bannepeš yᵉkappēr, "for the blood is what atones for the life" (Lev. 17:11H).

#365. Cj + <NSus,PrRes–(Ns <M> PpPh) >

kī bāttē 'ārē halᵉwiyyīm hī' 'ăḥuzzātām bᵉtōk bᵉnē yiśrā'ēl, "for the houses of the cities of the Levites—it is their possession in the midst of the sons of Israel" (Lev. 25:33H).

#366. Cj + <NSus,PrRes–Ni>

kī kol-hā'ēdā kullām qᵉdōšīm, "for all the community—all of them are holy" (Num. 16:3P). Compare Isa. 60:21.

#367. Subordinate declarative verbless clause with core <SSus, SRes–P> plus margin

#367. Cj + PpPh + <NdSus,PrRes–PpPh>

kī kahaṭṭā't hā'āšām hū' lakkōhēn, "for, like the sin offering, the guilt offering is the priest's" (Lev. 14:13P).

#368-401. Subordinate declarative verbless clauses with core <P–S> and no margins

#368. Cj + <Pr–Pr>

kī-hū' ze, "that this is it" (Exod. 22:8C). Compare #322.

#369. Cj + < (N <Ct> Np)–Pr>

kī ben-ribqā hū', "that he is Rebekah's son" (Gen. 29:12J). Other examples: Gen. 22:12E; Deut. 7:25; 17:1; 23:19. Compare Judg. 6:22; 13:16, 21; I Sam. 24:7, 11; Mal. 2:7.

#370. Cj + < (N <Ct> Nd)–Pr>

kī-ṣārebet hammikwā hī' "for it is the scar of the burn" (Lev. 13: 28P.)

#371. Cj + <Ns–Pr>

kī 'āḥīkā hū', "for he is your brother" (Deut. 23:8). Other examples: Gen. 12:18J; 21:13E; 37:27J; 38:16L; Exod. 21:21C; Lev. 18: 10H; 22:7H; Num. 14:9P. Compare Judg. 9:2, 18.

#372. Cj + <(N <Ct> Ns)–Pr>

kī 'āḥī 'ābīhā hū', "that he is her father's brother" (Gen. 29:12J). Another example: Lev. 18:13H.

#373. Cj + <Pti–Pr>

kī bōrēḥ hū', "that he is fleeing" (Gen. 31:20J). Other examples: Gen. 29:33J; Num. 22:12E, 22J. Similarly: Deut. 14:8. Compare Jer. 10:16.

#374. Cj + <Ni–Pr>

kī-ḥannūn 'ānī, "for I am compassionate" (Exod. 22:26C). Other examples: Gen. 3:7L, 10L, 11L, 19J; 6:2L; 20:7E; 25:21J, 30J [compare Judg. 8:5]; 29:9J; 42:16E, 19E, 33E, 34E; Exod. 1:16E, 16E, 19L; 2:2L; 5:8J; 9:32J; 13:17L; 15:23J; 22:14C; 29:28P, 33P, 34P; 32:25L; 34:10J; Lev. 5:11P; 11:42P, 44P, 45P; 13:11P; 14:21P; 25:12H; 27:4P; Num. 15:25P; 22:3E; Deut. 7:26; 24:15. Similarly: Lev. 19:2H; 20: 26H; 21:8H.

#375. Cj + <(Ni <A> Ni)–Pr>

'im-'īš 'ānī hū', "if he is a poor man" (Deut. 24:12). Other examples: Gen. 12:11J; 13:8J. Compare Jos. 24:19; Judg. 11:2.

#376. Cj + <(N <Ct> Ni)–Pr>

'im ba'al 'iššā hū', "if he is the husband of a wife" (Exod. 21:3C). Other examples: Gen. 26:7J [compare Est. 1:11]; Exod. 4:10E; 29:22P; 33:3J; 34:9J; Lev. 10:12P, 17P; 11:4P, 5P, 6P, 7P; 13:28P, 52P; Deut. 9:6; 14:7; 23:19; 32:28. Compare Jos. 17:15; I Sam. 20:31; 26:16.

#377. Cj + <PpPh–Pr>

kī-'ittᵉkā 'ānōkī, "for I am with you" (Gen. 26:24J). Another example: Exod. 32:22E.

#378. Cj + <Pti–Np>

kī šōmē' yōsēp, "that Joseph is understanding" (Gen. 42:23E). Another example: Gen. 29:31J.

#379.* Cj + <Ni–Np>

kī ṭōb yahwe, "for YHWH is good" (Jer. 33:11).

#380. Cj + <(Ni <A> Ni)–(Np <A> Ns)>

kī 'ēl raḥūm yahwe 'ĕlōheykā, "for YHWH your god is a merciful god" (Deut. 4:31). Compare Jos. 10:2; I Sam. 2:3; Hos. 11:1.

#381.* Cj + <Ni–(N <Ct> Np) >
kī-yāšār dᵉbar-yahwe, "for YHWH's word is straight" (Ps. 33:4).
Other examples: Isa. 13:6; Joel 1:15; 4:14; Obad. 15; Zeph. 1:7, 14.
Compare II Kings 22:13.

#382. Cj + <Ni–(N <Ct> N <Ct> Np) >
kī ʿaz gᵉbūl bᵉnē ʿammōn, "for the boundary of the Ammonites is
strong" (Num. 21:24E).

#383. Cj + <Ns–(Nd <A> Nd) >
kī ʿammᵉkā haggōy hazze, "for this nation is your people" (Exod.
33:13J).

#384.* Cj + <PtiPh–Nd>
kī-nōgaʿat ʿᵃlēhem hārāʿā, "that the disaster was about to strike
them" (Judg. 20:34).

#385. Cj + <Ni–(Nd <A> PtdPh) >
kīʿaz hāʿām hayyōšēb bāʾareṣ, "but the people who dwells in the
land is strong" (Num. 13:28J).

#386. Cj + < (Ni <M> PpPh)–Nd>
kī-kābēd mimmᵉkā haddābār, "for the matter is too heavy for you"
(Exod. 18:18E).

#387. Cj + < (N <Ct> Ni)–Nd>
ʾim-bin hakkōt hārāšāʿ, "if the guilty man is due for beating" (Deut.
25:2). Compare II Sam. 12:5.

#388. Cj + <PpPh–Nd>
kī-lī hāʾareṣ, "for the earth is mine" (Lev. 25:23H). Other examples: Exod. 9:29J; Lev. 27:27P.

#389. Cj + <PpPh–(N <Ct> Nd) >
kī-lī kol-hāʾareṣ, "for all the earth is mine" (Exod. 19:5E).

#390. Cj + <Np–Ns>
kī śārā šᵉmāh, "for her name is Sarah" (Gen. 17:15P).

#391.* Cj + <Pti–Ns>
kī šōmēʿ ʿabdekā, "for your slave is listening" (I Sam. 3:9, 10).
Compare Isa. 12:4.

#392. Cj + <Ni–Ns>
ʾim-ʿōlā qorbānō, "if his offering is a burnt offering" (Lev. 1:3P).
Other examples: Lev. 3:12P; Num. 6:12P. Compare II Sam. 17:10;
19:27; 24:14; Jer. 4:22; 10:14.

#393. Cj + < (Ni <M> PpPh) –Ns>
'im-minḥā 'al-hammaḥăbat qorbānekā, "if your offering is a cereal offering cooked on a pan" (Lev. 2:5P).

#394. Cj + < (N <Ct> Ni) –Ns>
'im-minḥat marḥešet qorbānekā, "if your offering is a gift of cooked cereal" (Lev. 2:7P). Another example: Lev. 3:1P. Compare Isa. 26:19.

#395. Cj + < (Part <A> Ni) – (Ns <M> PpPh) >
'im-min hā'ōp 'ōlā qorbānō lᵉyahwe, "if his offering for YHWH is any bird as a burnt offering" (Lev. 1:14P).

#396. Cj + <Ni– (N <Ct> Ns) >
kī-qārōb yōm 'ēdām, "for the day of their calamity is near" (Deut. 32:35). Similarly: Lev. 7:16P.

#397. Cj + < (N <Ct> Np) –Pti>
kī-qilᵉlat 'ĕlōhīm tālūy, "for a hanged person is cursed by God" (Deut. 21:23).

#398. Cj + < (N <Ct> Np) – (N <Ct> N <Ct> Ni) >
kī-tō'ăbat miṣrayim kol-rō'ē ṣō'n, "for every shepherd is an abomination to Egypt" (Gen. 46:34J). Other examples: Deut. 18:12; 22:5: 25:16.

#399. Cj + <PpPh– (N <Ct> Ni) >
kī lī kol-bᵉkōr, "for every firstborn is mine" (Num. 3:13P). Another example: Num. 8:17P.

#400. Cj + < (Ni <M> PpPh)) –IfPh>
kī ṭōb bᵉ'ēnē yahwe lᵉbārēk 'et-yiśrā'ēl, "that to bless Israel is good in the eyes of YHWH" (Num. 24:1E).

#401. Cj + <PpPh–PpPh>
kī kāmōkā kᵉpar'ō, "for like Pharaoh is like you" (Gen. 44:18J).

##402-407. Subordinate declarative verbless clauses with core <P–S> plus margins

#402. Cj + Neg + <Ni–Pr>
kī lō' mᵉraggᵉlīm 'attem, "that you are not spies" (Gen. 42:34E). Compare I Sam. 15:29, which Albrecht (p. 220) considers abnormal; but see Num. 23:19.

#403. Cj + Neg + < (N <Ct> Ni) –Pr>
kī lō'-'ēṣ ma'ăkāl hū', "that it is not a food tree" (Deut. 20:20).

#404.* Cj + Neg + <Ni–(Nd <A> Nom)>

kī lō'-ṭōbā haššᵉmū'ā 'ăšer 'ānōkī šōmē', "for the report I hear is not good" (I Sam. 2:24).

#405. Cj + Neg + <PpPh–Nd>

kī lō' kannāšīm hammiṣriyyōt hā'ībriyyōt, "for the Hebrew women are not like the Egyptian women" (Exod. 1:19E).

#406. Cj + Neg + <PpPh–Ns>

kī lō' kᵉṣūrēnū ṣūrām, "for their rock is not like our rock" (Deut. 32:31).

#407. Cj + Adv + <PpPh–Ni>

kī-gam-ze lāk bēn, "for now also you have a son" (Gen. 35:17E)

#408-428. Subordinate declarative verbless clauses with core <P...–S ...P> with no margins

#408.* Cj + < (N <Ct> Np)...–Pr ...PpPh>

kī-nᵉzīr 'ĕlōhīm 'ănī mibbeṭen 'immī, "for I am a nazir of God from my mother's belly" (Judg. 16:17).

#409. Cj + <Ns...–Pr ...<A> Nom>

kī-'ăbāday hēm 'ăšer-hōṣē'tī 'ōtām mē'ereṣ miṣrāyim, "for they are my slaves whom I brought from the land of Egypt" (Lev. 25:42H). Similarly: Lev. 10:13P.

#410. Cj + <Pti...–Pr ...<M> Md>

kī yārē' 'ānōkī 'ōtō, "for I fear him" (Gen. 32:12J; compare Dan. 1:10). Other examples: Gen. 19:13J; Exod. 7:27J; 9:2J; 10:4J (compare Jer. 38:21); Num. 25:18L; Deut. 5:22. Compare I Sam. 3:13.

#411. Cj + <Ni...–Pr ...<M> Adv>

kī-kābēd hū' mᵉ'ōd, "for it is very heavy" (Gen. 41:31J). Another example: Gen. 12:14J. Compare Gen. 47:13.

#412. Cj + <Ni...–Pr ...<M> PpPh>

kī-ḥerpā hī' lānū, "for it is a disgrace for us" (Gen. 34:14L). Other examples: Gen. 3:6L; 43:32J; Exod. 21:29C, 36C; 31:13P, 14P; Lev. 21:7H; 25:23H; 27:8P; Num. 8:16P; 13:31L; 18:31P; 22:6J; Deut. 7:6, 16; 14:2, 21; 24:4. Compare I Sam. 15:17; Jos. 9:16; Judg. 18:26.

#413. Cj + < (N <Ct> Ni)...–Pr ...<A> NiPh>

kī dōr tahpūkōt hēmmā bānīm lō'-'ēmūn bām, "for they are a perverse generation, sons with no reliability in them" (Deut. 32:20). Other examples: Gen. 37:3J; Exod. 4:25J; Lev. 11:7P; 13:4P; 23:28H; 24:9H; 25:34H; Num. 5:15P.

#414. Cj + <PpPh...–Pr ...<C> PpPh>

'im 'al-hammiškāb hū' 'ō 'al-hakkeli 'ăšer-hī' yōšebet-'ālāyw, "if he is on the bed or on the furniture that she sits on" (Lev. 15:23P).

#415. Cj + <Pti...–Np ...<M> Md>

kī-mašḥīt yahwe 'ēt-hā'īr, "because YHWH is destroying the city" (Gen. 19:14J). Other examples: Gen. 3:5L; 27:46P; Deut. 13:4. Compare: I Sam. 3:20; 23:10; 25:4; II Sam. 17:10; Jer. 25:36; 47:4; 51:55; Ruth 3:11.

#416. Cj + <Ni...–Np ...<M> PpPh>

kī-gādōl yahwe mikkol-hā'ĕlōhīm, "that YHWH is the greatest of all gods" (Exod. 18:11E). Another example: Deut. 6:15. Compare Jos. 10:2.

#417. Cj + <Ni...– (N <Ct> Np) ...<M> PpPh>

kī rā'ōt benōt kenā'an be'ēnē yiṣḥāq 'ābīw, "that the daughters of Canaan are evil in the eyes of Isaac his father" (Gen. 28:8P).

#418. Cj + <PpPh...– (N <Ct> Np) ...<M> Ni>

kī-lī benē yiṣrā'ēl 'ăbādīm, "for the sons of Israel are mine as slaves" (Lev. 25:55H).

#419. Cj + <Pti...–Nd ...<M> PpPh>

kī-nākōn haddābār mē'im hā'ĕlōhīm, "for the matter is settled from God" (Gen. 41:32E).

#420. Cj + <Ni...–Nd ...<M> Adv>

kī-kābēd hārā'āb me'ōd, "because the famine is very severe" (Gen. 47:13J).

#421. Cj + <Ni...–Nd ...<M> PpPh>

kī-kābēd hārā'āb bā'āreṣ, "for the famine is severe in the land" (Gen. 12:10J). Other examples: Gen. 3:6L; 47:4J; Exod. 16:25P. Similarly Deut. 30:14. Compare II Sam. 19:43. Contrast I Kings 19:7.

#422. Cj + <Ni...– (N <Ct> Nd) ...<M> PpPh>

kī rabbā rā'at hā'ādām bā'āreṣ, "how great in the earth is the evil of men" (Gen. 6:5L).

#423.* Cj + <Pti...–Ns ...<M> PpPh>

kī-meqaṭṭerōt nešēhem lē'lōhim 'ăḥērīm, "that their wives are offering incense to other gods" (Jer. 44:15).

#424. Cj + <Ni...–Ns ...<M> PpPh>

'im-'ōlā qorbānō min-habbāqār, "if his offering is a burnt offering from the herd" (Lev. 1:3P).

#425. Cj + <PpPh...–Ns ...<C> PpPh>

kī-miggepen sᵉdōm gapnām ūmiššadmōt ʿᵃmōrā, "for their vine is from the vine of Sodom and from the fields of Gomorrah" (Deut. 32: 32).

#426. Cj + <PpPh...–Ns ...<A> Ni>

ʾim-min-haṣṣōʾn qorbānō lᵉzebaḥ šᵉlāmīm lᵉyahwe zākār ʾō nᵉqēbā, "if his offering for a peace sacrifice for YHWH is from the flock, a male or a female" (Lev. 3:6P). Similarly: Lev. 1:10P.

#427.* Cj + <Ni...–(N <Ct> Ni) ...PpPh>

kī-rabbīm bᵉnē-šōmēmā mibbᵉnē bᵉʿūlā, "for the sons of the desolate are more numerous than the sons of the married" (Isa. 54:1).

#428. Cj + <(Ni <M> PpPh)...–IfPh ...<M> PpPh>

kī ṭōb lānū ʿᵃbōd ʾet-miṣrayim mimmūtēnū bammidbār, "for to serve Egypt is better for us than to die in the desert" (Exod. 14:12E).

##429-431. Subordinate declarative verbless clauses with core <P ...–S ...P> plus margins

#429. Cj + Neg + <Pti...–Pr ...<M> PpPh>

kī lōʾ śōnēʾ hūʾ lō mittᵉmōl šilšōm, "for he does not hate him previously" (Deut. 19:6). Compare Jos. 20:5.

#430. Cj + Neg + <(Ni <A> Ni)...–Pr ...<M> PpPh>

kī lōʾ-dābār rēq hūʾ mikkem, "for it is not a matter too trivial for you" (Deut. 32:47). Compare I Kings 19:4.

#431. Cj + Neg + <Ni...–Ns ...<M> PpPh>

ʾim-lōʾ qārōb ʾāḥīkā ʾēleykā, "if your brother is not near to you" (Deut. 22:2).

##432-435. Subordinate declarative verbless clauses with core <SSus,P–SRes>

#432. Cj + <NpSus,(N <Ct> Np)–PrRes>

kī ḥešbōn ʿīr sīḥōn melek hāʾᵉmōrī hīʾ, "for Heshbon is the capital of Sihon, king of the Amorites" (Num. 21:26E).

#433. Cj + <(Np <A> Nom)Sus,(Ni <A> Ni)–PrRes>

kī yahwe qannāʾ šᵉmō ʾēl qannāʾ hūʾ, "for YHWH, whose name is Passionate, he is a passionate god" (Exod. 34:14J).

#434. Cj + <(Nd <A> Nom)Sus,(N <Ct> Ni)–PrRes>

kī hammāqōm ʾᵃšer ʾattā ʿōmēd ʿālāyw ʾadmat-qōdeš hūʾ "for the place that you are standing on is holy ground" (Exod. 3:5J). Compare Jos. 5:15; Ezek. 3:7.

#435. Cj + <NdSus,PpPh–PrRes>

kī hammišpāṭ lē'lōhīm hū', "for the decision is God's" (Deut. 1:17).
Other examples: Gen. 45:20J; Lev. 17:11H, 14H.

#436-437. Subordinate declarative verbless clauses with core <SSus,P...–SRes ...P>

#436. Cj + <NpSus, (Ni <A> Ni) –PrRes...<A> (Ni <A> Ni) >

kī yahwe 'ĕlōheykā 'ēš 'ōkᵉlā hū' 'ēl qannā', "for YHWH your god
is a devouring fire, a passionate god" (Deut. 4:24). Similarly: Deut.
30:11. Compare II Sam. 21:2.

#437. Cj + <[(N <Ct> Nd) <A> Nom],PpPh–PrRes ...<C>
      PpPh>

kī kol-hā'ōšer 'ăšer hiṣṣīl 'ĕlōhīm mē'ābīnū lānū hū' ūlᵉbānēnū,
"for all the wealth that God took from our father is ours and our children's" (Gen. 31:16E). Similarly: Deut. 11:10.

#438. Subordinate declarative verbless clause with core <PSus,
PRes–S>

#438. Cj + <PpPhSus,AdvRes–(Nd <A> Nd) >

kī ka'ăšer yāqūm 'īš 'al-rē'ēhū ūrᵉṣāḥō nepeš kēn haddābār hazze,
"for as when someone rises up against someone else and murders him,
so is this business" (Deut. 22:26). Compare I Sam. 25:25.

#439. Subordinate declarative verbless clause with core <P...–S
......P ...S>

#439. Cj + <PpPh...–Ns... ...<A> PpPh ...<M> PpPh>

'im-min-haṣṣō'n qorbānō min hakkᵉśābīm 'ō min-hā'izzīm lᵉ'ōlā, "if
his offering for burnt sacrifice is from the flock, from the sheep or
from the goats" (Lev. 1:10P).

#440-459. Nominalized verbless declarative clauses with core <S–P> and no margins

#440. Nom + <Pr–Ns>

'ăšer 'attᵉ-'ištō, "that you are his wife" (Gen. 39:9J).

#441. Nom + <Pr–Pti>

'ăšer 'ănī 'ōśe, "that I am doing" (Gen. 18:17J). Other examples:
Gen. 13:15L; 21:22E; 28:20E; 31:43E; 34:22J; 39:3J, 6J, 23J, 23J;
47:14J; Exod. 18:17E; 36:4P.

#442. Nom + <Pr–(Pti <M> Md) >

'ăšer 'ănī dōbēr 'ēleykā, "which I am saying to you" (Exod. 6:29P).

Other examples: Gen. 9:12P; 24:3J, 37J, 42J; 27:8J; 28:13J; Exod.
3:5J; 5:8J; 16:8P; 18:5E, 14E, 14E; 25:9P, 40P; 34:10J, 11J, 12J; Lev.
11:26P; 14:34P; 15:23P; 17:5H, 7H; 18:3H, 24H; 20:22H, 23H; 22:2H;
23:10H; 25:2H; Num. 5:3P; 13:19J, 19J; 14:8P, 27P, 27P; 15:2P, 18P,
39P; 17:20P; 18:21P; 33:55P; 35:34P, 34P; Deut. 3:21; 4:1, 2, 2, 5, 8, 14,
26, 40; 5:1, 28; 6:1, 2, 2, 6, 8; 7:1, 11, 19; 8:1, 11; 9:12; 10:13; 11:8,
8, 10, 11, 13, 22, 27, 28, 29, 32; 12:2, 8, 11, 14, 28, 29; 13:1, 19; 15:5;
18:6, 14; 19:9; 20:20; 23:21; 24:11; 27:1, 4, 10; 28:1, 13, 14, 15, 21, 52, 63;
30:2, 8, 11, 16, 16, 18, 18; 31:13, 16, 21; 32:46, 47, 49, 50, 52.

#443. Nom + <Pr–Ni>
'ăšer hū' ṭāhōr, "who is clean" (Num. 9:13P) . Another example:
Gen. 9:3P.

#444. Nom + <Pr–(Ni <M> PpPh) >
'ăšer hēm ḥayyīm 'al-hā'ădāmā, "that they live on the earth" (Deut.
4:10; compare I Kings 8:40, II Chr. 6:31) . Other examples: Num. 35:
31P; Deut. 12:1; 31:13. Compare Ruth 4:15; Neh. 2:18.

#445. Nom + <Pr–Adv>
'ăšer-'attā šām, "where you are" (Gen. 13:14L; compare I Sam. 19:
3) . Other examples: Gen. 21:17E; Exod. 12:13P.

#446. Nom + <Pr–PpPh>
'ăšer 'ānōkī beqirbō, "which I am in the midst of" (Num. 11:21J) .
Other examples: Gen. 38:25L; Exod. 8:17J; 34:10J; Num. 35:33P.
Similarly: Lev. 11:39P.

#447. Nom + <Np–Pti>
'ăšer hā'ĕlōhīm 'ōśe, "which God is doing" (Gen. 41:25E, 28E) .

#448. Nom + <Np–(Pti <M> Md) >
'ăšer yahwe nōtēn lākem, "which YHWH is giving you" (Deut. 11:
17) . Other examples: Gen. 31:12E; 40:3E; Exod. 3:9E; 6:5P; 20:12E;
Deut. 1:20, 25; 2:29; 3:20; 4:1, 21, 40; 5:16; 7:16; 8:20; 11:12, 31;
12:9, 10; 13:13; 15:4, 7; 16:5, 18, 20; 17:2, 14; 18:9; 19:1, 2, 10, 14; 20:
16; 21:1, 23; 24:4; 25:15, 19; 26:1, 2; 27:2, 3; 28:8; 29:12.

#449. Nom + <Np–PpPh>
'ăšer yahwe 'ittō, "that YHWH is with him" (Gen. 39:23J) .

#450. Nom + < (N <Ct> Np) –PpPh>
'ăšer rūḥ 'ĕlōhīm bō, "in whom is the spirit of God" (Gen. 41:38E) .

#451. Nom + <Nd–PpPh>
'ăšer hannega‘ bō, "which the disease is in" (Lev. 13:46P) .

#452. Nom + < (N <Ct> Nd) –Np>
'ăšer šēm hā'aḥat šiprā, "of whom the name of the one is Shiphrah" (Exod. 1:15L). Another example: Exod. 18:3J.

#453. Nom + < (N <Ct> Nd) –Pti>
'ăšer-'ăsīrē hammelek 'ăsūrīm, "where the king's prisoners are bound" (Gen. 39:20J).

#454. Nom + <Ns–Pti>
'ăšer 'ădōnī dōbēr, "which my master says" (Num. 32:27J). Another example: Num. 32:25J).

#455. Nom + <Ns– (Pti <M> Md) >
'ăšer 'ammī 'ōmēd 'āleyhā, "which my people are standing on" (Exod. 8:18J). Another example: Deut. 29:17.

#456. Nom + <Ns–Ni>
'ăšer 'ăbāneyhā barzel, "whose stones are iron" (Deut. 8:9).

#457. Nom + <Ns–PpPh>
'ăšer zar'ō-bō, "whose seed is in it" (Gen. 1:11P, 12P).

#458. Nom + <Ni–PpPh>
'ăšer lābān bō, "in which is white" (Gen. 30:35J). Another example: Num. 27:18P.

#459. Nom + < (N <Ct> N <Ct> Ni) –PpPh>
'ăšer nišmat-rūḥ ḥayyīm be'appāyw, "in whose nostrils is the breath of the air of life" (Gen. 7:22J).

 # #460-469. Nominalized declarative verbless clauses with core <P–S> and no margins

#460. Nom + <Adv–Np>
'ăšer-šām hā'ĕlōhīm, "where God is" (Exod. 20:21E).

#461. Nom + <Adv– (N <Ct> Np) >
'ăšer-šām benē yiśrā'ēl, "where the sons of Israel are." (Exod. 9:26J). Compare I Sam. 3:3; 10:5; I Kings 8:21=II Chr. 6:11.

#462. Nom + <Adv–Nd>
'ăšer-šām hazzāhāb, "where the gold is" (Gen. 2:11J). Compare I Sam. 9:10; Ezek. 8:3.

#463. Nom + <PpPh–Nd>
'ăšer lāhem hārīb, "who have the quarrel" (Deut. 19:17). Other examples: Gen. 38:30L; Lev. 13:45P, 54P, 57P; 14:35P, 40P.

#464. Nom + <PpPh-(N <Ct> Nd) >
'ăšer-lō 'ăḥuzzat hā'āreṣ, "who has the land tenure" (Lev. 27:24P).

#465. Nom + <Np–Ns>
[*kī yahwe*] *qannō' šemō,* "[for YHWH] (whose) name is Passionate" (Exod. 34:14J). Compare Job 1:1; Zech. 6:12. See p. 41.

#466. Nom + <PpPh–Ni>
'ăšer-lō 'orlā, "who has a foreskin" (Gen. 34:14J). Other examples: Lev. 11:9P; 21:18H, 21H; 22:20H; Deut. 14:9.

#467. Nom + <PpPh-(Ni <M> PpPh) >
'ăšer-lō 'ĕlōhīm qerōbīm 'ēlāyw keyahwe 'ĕlōhēnū. . . , "which has gods near it like YHWH our god . . ." (Deut. 4:7). Other examples: Lev. 11:21P; Deut. 4:8.

#468. Nom + <PpPh-(N <Ct> Ni) >
'ăšer-bō nepeš ḥayyā, "in which is life-soul" (Gen. 1:30P). Other examples: Gen. 1:29P; 6:17P; 7:15P; Lev. 14:32P.

#469. Nom + <PpPh–Num>
'ăšer-lō 'arba' raglāyim, "which has four legs" (Lev. 11:23P).

##470-473. Nominalized declarative verbless clauses with core <P–S> plus margins

#470. Nom + Neg + <Ns–Pr>
'ăšer lō'-'āḥīkā hū', "who is not your brother" (Deut. 17:15).

#471. Nom + Md + <Pti–Pr> + Voc
'ăšer-'ayin be'ayin nir'ā 'attā yahwe, "that you, YHWH, are seen eye to eye" (Num. 14:14J).

#472. Nom + Neg + <Ni–Pr>
'ăšer lō' ṭehōrā hī', "which is not clean" (Gen. 7:2J).

#473. Nom + Neg + <Part–Pr>
'ăšer lō' mizzera' 'ăhărōn hū', "who is not one of Aaron's progeny" (Num. 17:5P). Other examples: Gen. 17:12P; Deut. 20:15.

##474-478. Independent precative verbless clauses with core <S–P> and no margins

#474. <Ns–Pti>
'ōrereykā 'ārūr, "let those who curse you be cursed" (Gen. 27:29J). Other examples: Num. 24:9J; Deut. 28:31, 31, 31, 32.

#475. <Ns–PpPh>
dāmāyw bō, "let his blood be against him" (Lev. 20:9H). Other

examples: Gen. 16:5J, 12J; 49:8L; Lev. 20:11H, 12H, 13H, 16H, 27H.

#476. <Ni–PpPh>

šālōm lākem, "may you have peace" (Gen. 43:23J). Other examples: Gen. 18:25J; Exod. 22:2C; Num. 15:31P; 16:3P; Deut. 3:26.

#477. < (N <Ct> Ni) –PpPh>

kol-peṭer reḥem lī, "let every firstborn be mine" (Exod. 34:19J). Another example: Lev. 3:16P.

#478. <Num–PpPh>

tōrā 'aḥat lāhem, "let them have one rule" (Lev. 7:7P).

##479-481. Independent precative verbless clauses with core <S–P> plus margins

#479. <Np–PpPh> + PpPh

'ĕlōhīm 'imm^ekā b^ekōl 'ăšer-'attā 'ōśe, "may God be with you in all that you do" (Gen. 21:22E). Another example: Exod. 10:10J.

#480. <Ni–PpPh> + Voc

'ōy-l^ekā mō'āb, "woe to you, Moab" (Num. 21:29E).

#481. <Ni–PpPh> + Adv

ḥag l^eyahwe māḥār, "let there be a festival for YHWH tomorrow" (Exod. 32:5J). Another example: Exod. 16:23P.

#482. Independent precative verbless clauses with core <S...–P...S>

#482. <Ni...–PpPh ...PpPh>

ḥālīlā llī mē'ăśōt zō't, "let me have a curse for doing this" (Gen. 44:17J). Other examples: Gen. 18:25J; 44:7J; Exod. 17:16L.

#483. Independent precative verbless clause with core <PSus,S...–PRes ...S>

#483. <NdSus,Num...–PpPh[PrRes] ...<A> NPh>

haqqāhāl ḥuqqā 'aḥat lākem w^elaggēr haggār 'ōlām l^edōrōtēkem, "the assembly, let one statute be for you and for the alien who sojourns, a perpetual statute through your generations" (Num. 15:15P).

##484-491. Independent precative verbless clauses with core <P–S> and no margins

#484. <Pti–Np>

'ārūr k^enā'an, "cursed be Canaan" (Gen. 9:25L). Other examples: Gen. 9:26L; 24:27J; Exod. 18:10J. Similarly: Deut. 33:24.

#485. <Pti–(Nd <A> Nom)>
'ārūr hā'īš 'ăšer ya'ăśe pesel ūmassēkā tō'ăbat yahwe ma'ăśē y^edē ḥārāš, "cursed be the man who makes a carved or cast image, an abomination to YHWH, a craftsman's handiwork" (Deut. 27:15).

#486. <Pti–(Nd <A> Nd)>
'ēd haggal hazze, "let this heap witness" (Gen. 31:52L).

#487. <Pti–Nom>
'ārūr 'ăšer lō'-yāqīm 'et-dibrē hattōrā-hazzō't la'ăśōt 'ōtām, "cursed be he who does not uphold the contents of this instruction by doing them" (Deut. 27:26).

#488. <Pti–NsPh>
bārūk ṭan'ăkā ūmiš'artekā, "may your basket and your kneading trough be blessed" (Deut. 28:5). Another example: Deut. 28:17. Similarly: Gen. 49:7L; Deut. 33:13.

#489. <PpPh–Ns>
miḥūṣ lammaḥăne mōšābō, "let his residence be outside the camp" (Lev. 13:46P).

#490. <Pti–(N <Ct> Ns) Ph>
'ārūr p^erī-biṭn^ekā ūp^erī 'admātekā. . . , "cursed be the fruit of your body and the fruit of your ground" (Deut. 28:18). Another example: Deut. 28:4.

#491. <Pti–PtiPh>
'ārūr maqle 'ābīw w^e'immō, "cursed be he who dishonors his father and his mother" (Deut. 27:16). Other examples: Deut. 27:17, 18, 19, 20, 21, 22, 23, 24, 25; 33:20.

#492. Independent precative verbless clause with core <P–S> plus margin

#492. <PpPh–Ns> + Voc
'ālay qil^elātekā b^enī, "may your curse be upon me, my son" (Gen. 27:13J).

##493-495. Independent precative verbless clauses with core <P ...–S ...P> and no margins

#493. <Pti...–Pr ...<M> PpPh>
bārūk 'attā bā'īr, "may you be blessed in the city" (Deut. 28:3). Other examples: Gen. 3:14L; Num. 3:9P; Deut. 28:6, 16, 19. Compare Judg. 17:2.

#494. <Pti...–Np ...<M> PpPh>

bārūk 'abrām le'ēl 'elyōn qōnē šāmayim wā'āreṣ, "may Abram be blessed by El Elyon, maker of sky and earth" (Gen. 14:19P).

#495. <Pti...Nd ...<M> PpPh>

'ărūrā hā'ădāmā ba'ăbūrekā, "may the ground be cursed on account of you" (Gen. 3:17J).

#496. Coordinate precative verbless clauses with core <S–P> and no margins

#496. w– + <Ns–Pti>

we'ōrăreykā 'ārūr, "and let those who curse you be cursed" (Num. 24:9J). Another example: Gen. 27:29J.

##497-498. Coordinate precative verbless clauses with core <P–S> and no margin

#497. w– + <Pti–(Np <A> Nom)>

ūbārūk 'ēl 'elyōn 'ăšer-miggēn ṣāreykā be'yādekā, "and blessed be El Elyon who delivered your enemies into your power" (Gen. 14:20P).

#498. w– + <Pti–Nd>

we'ēdā hammaṣṣēbā, "and let the pillar be witnessing" (Gen. 31:52J).

##499-500. Coordinate precative verbless clauses with core <P ...–S ...P> and no margins

#499. w– + <Pti...–Pr ...<M> PpPh>

ūbārūk 'attā baśśāde, "and may you be blessed in the country" (Deut. 28:3). Another example: Deut. 28:16.

#500. w– + <Pti...–Pr ...<M> IfPh>

we'ārūr 'attā be'ṣē'tekā, "and may you be cursed when you go out" (Deut. 28:19). Another example: Deut. 28:6.

#501. Coordinate precative verbless clause with core <P...–S ... P> plus margin

#501. w– + Adv + <Pti...–Pr ...<M> PpPh>

we'attā 'ārūr 'attā min-hā'ădāmā 'ăšer pāṣe'tā 'et-pīhā lāqaḥat 'et-de'mē 'aḥīkā miyyādekā, "and now, may you be more cursed than the ground which opened its mouth to receive your brother's blood from your hand" (Gen. 4:11J).

##502-514. Independent interrogative verbless clauses with core <P–S>, P=Int

#502. <Int–Pr>
mī-'āttā, "who are you?" (Gen. 27:32J). Other examples: Gen. 48: 8E; Exod. 13:14L; 16:15J; Num. 13:18J. Similarly: Gen. 23:15P (?) ; 27:18J, 33J; Exod. 3:11E.

#503. <PpInt–Pr>
lᵉmī 'attā, "whose are you?" (Gen. 32:18E). Other examples: Gen. 33:15J. Similarly: Gen. 25:22L; 29:4J.

#504. < (N <Ct> Int)–Pr>
bat-mī 'attᵉ, "whose daughter are you?" (Gen. 24:23J, 47J).

#505. <Int–(Np <A> Nom) >
mī yahwe 'ăšer 'ešmaʿ bᵉqōlō lᵉšallaḥ 'et-yiśrā'ēl, "who is YHWH whose voice I should heed to send Israel away?" (Exod. 5:2E). Compare Exod. 3:11E.

#506. <Int–(Nd <A> Nd) >
mī-hā'īš hayyārē', "who is the frightened man?" (Deut. 20:8). Other examples: Gen. 24:65J; 37:10J; 38:18L; 44:15J; Exod. 10:8J; 12:26L; 18:14E; Num. 22:9E; Deut. 6:20; 20:5.

#507. <PpInt–(Nd <C> Nd) >
lᵉmī haḥōtemet wᵉhappᵉtīlīm wᵉhammaṭṭe hā'ēlle, "whose are this seal and cord and staff?" (Gen. 38:25L).

#508. <Int–Numd>
mā hēnnā šᵉbaʿ kᵉbāśōt hā'ēlle 'ăšer hiṣṣabtā lᵉbaddānā, "what are these seven female lambs that you have put by themselves?" (Gen. 21:29E).

#509. <Int–Nom>
mī 'ăšer ḥāṭā'-lī, "who is he who has sinned against me?" (Exod. 32:33J).

#510. <Int–Ns>
ma ḥāṭṭā'tī, "what is my fault?" (Gen. 31:36J). Other examples: Gen. 29:15L; 31:36J; 32:28L; 46:33J; 47:3J; Exod. 3:13E.

#511. <PpInt–(N <Ct> N <Ct> Ns) >
kammā yᵉmē šᵉnē ḥayyeykā, "what are the days of the years of your life like?" (Gen. 47:8P).

#512. <Int–Ni> + Cl

ma-bbeṣaʿ kī nahărōg ʾet-ʾāḥīnū, "what advantage is it if we slay our brother?" (Gen. 37:26J). Other examples: Deut. 3:24; 4:7, 8.

#513. <Int–(N <Ct> Ni) >

mī baʿal dᵉbārīm, "who is an orator?" (Exod. 24:14J). Another example: Deut. 5:26.

#514. <Int–PpPh>

ma-bbabbāyit, "what is in the house?" (Gen. 39:8J). Other examples: Gen. 31:32E; 33:5E, 8J (compare Gen. 21:17; Exod. 12:26); Exod. 4:2L; 32:26L. Similarly: Gen. 21:17E; Exod. 15:11, 11; Deut. 33:29.

#515. Coordinate interrogative verbless clause with core <S–P>, P=Int

#515. w– + <Pr–Int>

wᵉnaḥnū mā, "and what are we?" (Exod. 16:8P). Similarly: Exod. 16:7P.

##516-519. Coordinate interrogative verbless clauses with core <P–S>, P=Int

#516. w– + <Int–Nd>

ūmā hāʾāreṣ, "and what is the land?" (Num. 13:20E). Other examples: Num. 13:19E, 19E; Deut. 20:6, 7.

#517. w– + <Int–[(Ni <A> Ni) <A> Nom]>

ūmī gōy gādōl ʾăšer-lō ḥuqqīm ūmišpāṭīm . . . , "and who is a great nation who has statutes and customs . . ." (Deut. 4:8).

#518. w– + <PpInt–(Pr <M> PpPh) >

ūlᵉmī ʾēlle lᵉpāneykā, "and whose are these before you?" (Gen. 32:18E).

#519. w– + <NpSus,Int–Pr> + Cl

wᵉʾahărōn ma-hūʾ kī tallīwnū ʿālāyw, "and Aaron, what is he that you murmur at him?" (Num. 16:11P).

##520-522. Independent interrogative verbless clauses with core <S–P> and no margins

#520. IntAdv + <Pr–Pti>

ʾēpō hēm rōʿīm, "where are they shepherding?" (Gen. 37:16J). Other examples: Exod. 18:14E; Num. 14:41J; Deut. 1:28. Compare Ezek. 8:6.

#521. Int + <Pr-[(Ns <A> Nd) <A> Nom]>

hăze 'ăḥīkem haqqāṭōn 'ăšer 'ămartem 'ēlāy, "is this your young brother whom you told me about?" (Gen. 43:29J). Another example: Gen. 27:21J. In Gen. 27:24 and II Sam. 16:17 similar questions lack *hă-.* Compare II Sam. 18:32 with II Sam. 18:29.

#522. Int + <Ni–PpPh>

hăšālōm lō, "is he well?" (Gen. 29:6J). Another example: Gen. 42: 16E. Compare Gen. 43:27J; II Sam. 18:29, 32.

##523-531. Independent interrogative verbless clauses with core <S–P> plus margins

#523. IntAdv + <Ns–Ni> + Adv

maddū' p^enēkem rā'īm hayyōm, "why are your faces bad today?" (Gen. 40:7E). Compare II Sam. 13:4.

#524. Int + Neg + <Pr–(Nd <A> Nom) >

hălō'-ze haddābār 'ăšer dibbarnū 'ēleykā b^emiṣrayim, "is not this the word that we spoke to you in Egypt?" (Exod. 14:12E).

#525. Int + Neg + <Pr–Nom>

hălō' ze 'ăšer yište 'ădōnī bō, "is not this what my master drinks with?" (Gen. 44:5J).

#526. Int + Neg + <Pr–Ns>

hălō'-hū' 'ābīkā qānekā, "is not he your father, your creator?" (Deut. 32:6). Another example: Num. 22:30J.

#527. Int + Neg + <Pr–PtiPh>

hălō'-hū' kāmūs 'immādī ḥātūm b^e'ōṣ^erōtāy, "is it not stored with me, sealed in my treasuries?" (Deut. 32:34).

#528. Int + Neg + <Pr–PpPh>

hălō'-hēmmā b^e'ēber hayyardēn, "are they not in Transjordan?" (Deut. 11:30). Another example: Deut. 3:11.

#529. Int + Neg + < (Np <A> Ns) –Nd>

hălō' 'ăhărōn 'āḥīkā hallēwī, "is not Aaron your brother the Levite?" (Exod. 4:14J).

#530. Int + Neg + < (N <Ct> Nd) –PpPh>

hălō' kol-hā'āreṣ l^epāneykā, "is not all the land before you?" (Gen. 13:9J).

#531. Int + Neg + <Ns–(Pti <M> PpPh) >

hălō' 'aḥeykā rō'īm biškem, "are not your brothers shepherding in Shechem?" (Gen. 37:13J).

**#532. Independent interrogative verbless clause with core <P...
S–...P> plus margin**

#532. Int + <Inf <M>... Pr–Pti> + PpPh
hǎlhorgēnī 'attā 'ōmēr ka'ǎšer hāragtā 'et-hammiṣrī, "are you looking
for a chance to kill me as you killed the Egyptian?" (Exod. 2:14J).

**#533. Independent interrogative verbless clause with core <SSus,
SRes–P> plus margin**

#533. Int + < (Ni <A> Num),PrRes–PpPh> + Voc
habrākā 'aḥat hī'-lᵉkā 'ābī, "do you have one blessing, my father?"
(Gen. 27:38E).

**##534-539. Independent interrogative verbless clauses with core
<P–S> and no margins**

#534. Int + <PpPh–Ni>
lāmmā llī ḥayyīm, "why do I have life?" (Gen. 27:46P). Another
example: Num. 11:13J.

#535. Int + <PtiPh–Pr>
hǎšōmēr 'āḥī 'ānōkī, "am I my brother's keeper?" (Gen. 4:9J).

#536.* Int + <Ni–Pr>
ha'eprātī 'attā, "are you an Ephrathite?" (Judg. 12:5).

#537. Int + <PpPh–Pr>
hǎtaḥat 'ĕlōhīm 'ānī, "am I instead of God?" (Gen. 50:19E). Simi-
larly Gen. 30:2E. Compare II Kings 5:7.

#538.* Int + <Ni–Np>
ha'ebed yiśrā'ēl, "is Israel a slave?" (Jer. 2:14).

#539. Int + <Ni–IfPh>
ham'aṭ qaḥtēk 'et-'īšī, "is your taking my husband a small thing?"
(Gen. 30:15). Compare I Kings 2:13 (compare I Sam. 16:4).

**##540-543. Independent interrogative verbless clauses with core
<P–S> plus margins**

#540. Int + Neg + <Ni–Pr>
hǎlō' miṣ'ār hī', "is it not little?" (Gen. 19:20J). Compare I Sam.
26:15.

#541. Int + Neg + <PpPh–Ni>
hǎlō' lē'lōhīm pitrōnīm, "do not interpretations belong to God?"
(Gen. 40:8E).

106

#542. Int + Neg + < (Ni <M> PpPh) –IfPh>
hălō' ṭōb lānū šub miṣrāymā, "is returning to Egypt not good for us?" (Num. 14:3P).

#543. Int + Adv + <Ns–Pr>
hăkī-'āḥī 'attā, "are you really my brother?" (Gen. 29:15L).

#544-548. Independent interrogative verbless clauses with core <P...–S ...P> and no margins

#544. Int + < (N <Ct> Ns)...–Pr ...<C> Neg>
hakkᵉtōnet binkā hī' 'im lō', "is it your son's robe or not?" (Gen. 37:32J).

#545. Int + <Pti...–Pr ...PpPh + Nom>
hamkasse 'ănī mē'abrāhām 'ăšer 'ănī 'ōśe, "am I concealing from Abraham what I am doing?" (Gen. 18:17J). Another example: Num. 11:29J. Compare II Sam. 10:3; 15:27 (but compare LXX); Ezek. 8:6.

#546. Int + <Ni...–Pr ...<C> Neg>
hăṭōbā hī' 'im-rā'ā, "is it good or bad?" (Num. 13:19E). Other examples: Num. 13:18E, 18E, 20E. Compare I Sam. 17:43.

#547. Int + <Ni...– (N <Ct> Nd) >...IfPh>
hā'ādām 'ēṣ haśśādē lābō' mippāneykā bammāṣār, "are wild trees men to be besieged by you?" (Deut. 20:19).

#548.* Int + < (Ni <A> Pti)...–Ns ...PpPh>
ha'ayiṭ ṣābū' naḥălātī lī, "is my inheritance a speckled bird of prey to me?" (Jer. 12:9). Contrast Jer. 31:20.

#549-551. Independent interrogative verbless clauses with core <P...–S ...P> plus margins

#549.* Int + Neg + < (N <Ct> Ni)...–Pr ...<M> PpPh>
hălō' ben-yᵉmīnī 'ānōkī miqqᵉṭannē šibṭē yiśrā'ēl, "am I not a Benjamite from the smallest of the tribes of Israel?" (I Sam. 9:21).

#550.* Int + Neg + <Ni...–Np ...<M> PpPh>
hălō'-'āḥ 'ēśāw lᵉya'ăqōb, "is not Esau a brother of Jacob?" (Mal. 1:2).

#551.* Int + Neg + <Ni...– (N <Ct> Np) ...<M> PpPh>
hălō' ṭōb 'ōlᵉlōt 'eprayim mibṣīr 'ăbī'ezer, "is not the grape gleaning of Ephraim better than the vintage of Abiezer?" (Judg. 8:2). Compare II Kings 5:12.

107

#552. Independent interrogative verbless clause with core <SSus, P–SRes> plus margin

#552. Int + Neg + <NsPhSus,PpPh–PrRes>
miqnēhem weqinyānām wekol-behemtām hălō' lānū hēm, "their cattle, their property, and all their beasts, are they not ours?" (Gen. 34:23E).

#553. Coordinate interrogative verbless clauses with core <P...S–...P> plus margins

#553. w– + Adv + Voc + <Int... Np–...PtiPh>
we'attā yiśrā'ēl mā yahwe 'ĕlōheykā šō'ēl mē'immāk kī 'im-leyir'ā 'et-yahwe 'ĕlōheykā. . . , "and now, Israel, what does YHWH your god ask from you except to revere YHWH your god . . ." (Deut. 10: 12). Similarly: Num. 14:3P.

#554. Coordinate interrogative verbless clause with core <SSus, SRes–P> and no margin

#554. w– + <PrSus, [Int] PrRes–Pti>
wa'ănī 'ānā 'ănī-bā', "and I, where am I going?" (Gen. 37:30).

#555. Coordinate interrogative verbless clause with core <P–S> and no margin

#555. w– + Int + <PpPh–Ni>
welāmmā-zze lī bekōrā, "and why do I have a birthright?" (Gen. 25:32J).

Part IV: Tables

Table 1

Categories of Subject and Predicate in Verbless Clauses

1. Pr = Pronoun
2. Np = Proper noun (person or place name)
3. N <Ct> Np = Construct phrase with proper noun
4. Nd = Definite noun (article plus noun)
5. N <Ct> Nd = Construct phrase with definite noun
6. Ptd = Definite participle
7. Numd = Definite numeral
8. Nom = Nominalized construction
9. Ns = Suffixed noun (N <Ct> pronoun suffix)
10. N <Ct> Ns = Construct phrase with suffixed noun
11. Pti (Ph) = Indefinite participle (phrase)
12. Ni = Indefinite noun
13. N <Ct> Ni = Construct phrase with indefinite noun
14. Numi = Indefinite numeral
15. Part = Partitive phrase (*min* + N)
16. If (Ph) = Infinitive (phrase)
17. Adv = Adverb
18. PpPh = Prepositional phrase
19. Int = Interrogative

Table 2

The Cores of Declarative Verbless Clauses

	Total	Ind	Co	Sub	Nom
Nucleus S–P					
Total	1251	457	462	123	209
Core:					
S–P	1109	400	407	93	209
S...–P ...S	70	29	39	2	—
P... S–...P	39	16	8	15	—
SSus,SRes–P	29	9	7	13	—
PSus,S–PRes	3	3	—	—	—
PSus,S...–PRes ...S See #483.					
SSus,P... SRes–...P	1	—	1	—	—
Total discontinuous	142	57	55	30	—
Nucleus P–S					
Total	606	261	110	202	33
Core:					
P–S	417	174	85	125	33
P...–S ...P	133	63	6	64	—
SSus,P–SRes	35	17	11	7	—
PSus,PRes–S	1	—	—	1	—
SSus,P...–SRes ...P	19	7	8	4	—
P...–S.. ...P ...S	1	—	—	1	—
Total discontinuous	189	87	25	77	—
Grand Total	1857	718	572	325	242

Table 3
Independent Declarative Verbless Clauses with Pronoun Subject and No Margins or Discontinuities

Predicate category	Core S–P ##1-27		Core P–S ##90-101	
1. Pronoun (Pr)	—		—	
2. Proper noun (Np)	80		—	
3. N <Ct> Np	61		4	
4. Definite noun (Nd)	35		—	
		223		8
5. N <Ct> Nd	32		4	
6. Definite participle (Ptd)	7		—	
7. Definite numeral (Numd)	—		—	
8. Nominalized construction (Nom)	8		—	
9. Suffixed noun (Ns)	12		14	
		13		19
10. N <Ct> Ns	1		5	
11. Indefinite participle (Pti)	10	10	—	
12. Indefinite noun (Ni)	4		56	
13. N <Ct> Ni	5		14	
14. Indefinite numeral (Numi)	—		1	
15. Partitive phrase (Part)	—	11	I	75
16. Infinitive phrase (IfPh)	—		—	
17. Adverb (Adv)	—		—	
18. Prepositional phrase (PpPh)	2		3	
Total		257		102

Table 4
Occurrences of Nuclei S–P and P–S When S Is Definite (Table 1, categories 1-8) in Declarative Verbless Clauses Including Margins and Discontinuities

Predicate Category	Ind S–P	Ind P–S	Co S–P	Co P–S	Sub S–P	Sub P–S	Nom S–P	Nom P–S	Total S–P	Total P–S
1. Pr	—	—	—	—	1	1	—	—	1	1
2. Np	97	1	50	1	26	—	2	—	175	2
3. N <Ct> Np	87	7	33	2	1	6	—	—	121	15
4. Nd	38	—	15	—	7	—	—	—	60	—
5. N <Ct> Nd	38	5	12	1	2	1	—	—	52	7
6. Ptd	7	—	1	—	6	—	—	—	14	—
7. Numd	—	—	—	—	—	—	—	—	—	—
8. Nom	8	1	4	—	1	—	—	—	13	1
Subtotals	275	14	115	4	44	8	2	—	436	26
9. Ns	18	20	11	1	6	12	1	1	36	34
10. N <Ct> Ns	2	5	4	—	1	2	—	—	7	7
11. Pti	36	5	56	2	35	20	177	1	304	28
12. Ni	20	115	47	21	3	85	6	1	76	222
13. N<Ct>Ni	12	32	10	2	—	30	—	—	22	64
14. Numi	13	14	29	5	—	—	—	—	42	19
15. Part	—	1	—	—	—	—	—	3	—	4
16. IfPh	—	—	—	—	—	—	—	—	—	—
17. Adv	—	2	—	1	—	1	3	3	3	7
18. PpPh	10	11	31	21	11	15	9	8	61	55
Totals	386	219	303	57	100	173	198	17	984	466

Table 5
Continuity and Discontinuity in Predicate Phrases in Declarative Verbless Clauses with Nucleus P–S

Phrase Construction	Independent		Coordinate		Subordinate		Total	
	Cont.	Disc.	Cont.	Disc.	Cont.	Disc.	Cont.	Disc.
Coordination	6	3	—	—	1	5	7	8
Apposition	8	9	1	2	5	8	14	19
Apposition of Nominalized	—	2	—	—	—	2	—	4
Modified Participle	—	4	1	1	1	13	2	18
Modification by Adverb	—	1	1	—	—	3	1	4
Modification by Prepositional Phrase	4	49	—	10	4	40	8	99
Totals	18	68	3	13	11	71	32	152

The addition of Gen. 49:3 (#160), with discontinuity in a construct phrase, brings the grand total to 153, in agreement with Table 2.

In each pair of columns the left-hand column records the number of times the construction is continuous in the predicate; the right-hand column records the number of times the construction is discontinuous in the predicate.

Table 6
Occurrences of Nuclei S–P and P–S in Precative Verbless Clauses

Predicate Category	S–P	P–S	Total
Participle Phrase	8	40	48
Prepositional Phrase	28	2	30
Totals	36	42	78

Table 7
Independent Declarative Verbless Clauses, Nucleus <S–P>, ##1-89

Core ---> Nucleus	S–P	S.–P.S	P.S.–P	SS,SR–P	PS,S–PR
Pr–Np ##1-3	80			#84 1	
Pr–N<Ct>Np ##4-9,61,62	65	##74,75 21			
Pr–Nd ##10-12,63	36			#85 2	
Pr–N<Ct>Nd ##13-16	32	##76-78 6			
Pr–Ptd #17	7				
Pr–Nom #18	8				
Pr–Ns ##19-21,64	14			#86 3	
Pr–N<Ct>Ns #22	1	#79 1			
Pr–Pti ##23,65	12		#81 13	#87 2	
Pr–Ni ##24*,25,66,67	6				
Pr–N<Ct>Ni #26	5				
Pr–PpPh ##27,68	3				
Np–Ns #28*					
Np–Pti ##29,69	5		#82 1		
Np–Ni ##30,31	5				
Np–N<Ct>Ni ##32,33	6				
Np–PpPh ##34,70	3				
N<Ct>Np–Np #35	11				
N<Ct>Np–Pti			#83 2		
N<Ct>Np–Ni #36	1				
N<Ct>Np–PpPh #71	1				
Nd–N<Ct>Np #37	1				
Nd–Ns #38	1				
Nd–Pti #39	1				
Nd–Ni #40	1				
Nd–N<Ct>Ni #40	1				
Nd–PpPh #41	2				
N<Ct>Nd–Np #42	5				
N<Ct>Nd–Pti #43	1				
N<Ct>Nd–Ni #44	7				
N<Ct>Nd–Num #45	13				
N<Ct>Nd–PpPh #46	1				
Ns–Np #47	1				
Ns–Ptd #48	2				
Ns–Pti ##49,72	2				
Ns–Ni #50	6				
Ns–N<Ct>Ni #51	1				
Ns–Num #52	34				
Ns–PpPh #73	2				
N<Ct>Ns–Pti #53	1				
N<Ct>Ns–Num #54	1				
N<Ct>Ns–PpPh #55	2				
Ni–Ni #56	1				
Ni–PpPh #57	3	#80 1			#89 3
N<Ct>Ni–Num #58	4			#88 1	
N<Ct>Ni–PpPh #59	1				
Num–PpPh #60	4				
Totals 457	400	29	16	9	3

Table 8
Independent Declarative Verbless Clauses, Nucleus <P–S>, #90-174.

Core ---> Nucleus	P–S	P.–S.P	SS,P–SR	SS,P.–SR.P
N<Ct>Np–Pr	##90,132* 4	#141 2	#162 1	
N<Ct>Nd–Pr	#91 4		#169 1	
Ns–Pr	##92,133 15	#142 3		
N<Ct>Ns–Pr	#93 5			
Pti–Pr		#143 3		
Ni–Pr	##94-96,134,135 59	##144-147, 160,161 37	##163,164 4	#171 4
N<Ct>Ni–Pr	##97,136 15	##148,149 8	#165 2	##172,173 2
Num–Pr	##98,137 2	#150 1	#166 5	
Part–Pr	#99 1			
Adv–Pr			#170 1	
PpPh–Pr	##100,101,138 4		#167 1	
Nom–Np	#102 1			
Pti–Np	#103*			
Ns–Np	#104 2			
Ni–Np	##105,106 2			
N<Ct>Ni–Np	#107 2	#151 1		
Ni–N<Ct>Np	#108*	#152*		
Np–Nd	#109 1			
Pti–Nd		#153 2		
Ni–Nd	##110*,111,112,139 7	#154 1		#174 1
N<Ct>Ni–Nd	#113 2			
Num–Nd	#114 3			
Adv–Nd	#115 1			
PpPh–Nd	#116 1			
Num–N<Ct>Nd	#117 3			
PpPh–N<Ct>Nd	#118 5			
Np–Ns	#119 1			
Ni–Ns	#120 5	#155 2	#168 2	
N<Ct>Ni–Ns	#121 2	#156 1		
Num–Ns	#122 17	#157*		
Part–Ns	#123 1			
Adv–Ns	#124 1			
PpPh–Ns	#125 1	#158 1		
Np–N<Ct>Ns	#126 1			
PpPh–Ni	##127,140 5			
PpPh–N<Ct>Ni	#128 3			
Ni–IfPh	#129 4	#159 1		
Num–PpPh	#130 1			
PpPh–PpPh	#131 3			
Totals 261	174	63	17	7

Table 9
Coordinate Declarative Verbless Clauses, Nucleus <S–P>, ##175-280

Core ---> Nucleus	S–P		S.–P.S		P.S–.P		SS,SR–P		SS,P.SR–.P	
Pr–Np							#274	2		
Pr–N<Ct>Np	##175,244	9	##255,256	18			#275	1		
Pr–Nd	##176,177,245	9	##257,270	3			#276	1		
Pr–N<Ct>Nd	##178,179	7	##258,259	4						
Pr–Ptd							#277	1		
Pr–Nom	#180	2	#260	2						
Pr–Ns	##181-183	6	##261,262	2			#278	1		
Pr–N<Ct>Ns	##184,246	2	#263	2						
Pr–Pti	##185,186	16	#264	1	#271	3			#280	1
Pr–Ni	#187	13								
Pr–N<Ct>Ni	#188	4								
Pr–Num							#279	1		
Pr–PpPh	#189	8								
Np–Pti	#190	12			#272	4				
Np–Ni	#191	6								
Np–Num	##192,247	11								
Np–PpPh	#193	3								
N<Ct>Np–Np	##194,200	38								
N<Ct>Np–Nd	#201	2								
N<Ct>Np–N<Ct>Nd	#195	1								
N<Ct>Np–Pti	##196,202	3								
N<Ct>Np–Ni	#197	3								
N<Ct>Np–Num	##198,203	7								
N<Ct>Np–PpPh	##199,204,248	5								
Ptd–Np	#205	1								
Ptd–N<Ct>Nd	#206	4								
Nd–N<Ct>Np	#207	1								
Nd–Ns	#208	2								
Nd–Pti	##209,249	13								
Nd–Ni	##210,250	17	#265	1						
Nd–N<Ct>Ni	#211	3								
Nd–Num	#212	2								
Nd–PpPh	##213,251	6								
N<Ct>Nd–Np	#214	9								
N<Ct>Nd–Pti	#215	3								
N<Ct>Nd–Ni	#216	7								
N<Ct>Nd–N<Ct>Ni	#217	3								
N<Ct>Nd–Num	#218	5	#266	3						
N<Ct>Nd–PpPh	##219,252	8	#267	1						

Table 9—continued

Core – – –>		S–P	S.–P.S		P.S.–.P		SS,SR–P	SS,P.SR–.P
Nucleus								
Ns–Np	#220	9						
Ns–Nd	#221	1						
Ns–Pti	#222	8	#268	1				
Ns–Ni	##223,224,253	18						
Ns–N<Ct>Ni	#225	1						
Ns–Num	#226	28						
Ns–Adv	#227	1						
Ns–PpPh	#228	17	#269	1				
N<Ct>Ns–Np	#229	7						
N<Ct>Ns–Ni	##230,254	3						
N<Ct>Ns–PpPh	#231	1						
Ni–Np	#232	12						
Ni–Pti	#233	1			#273	1		
Ni–Num	#234	6						
Ni–PpPh	#235	10						
N<Ct>Ni–Np	#236	3						
N<Ct>Ni–Num	#237	2						
N<Ct>Ni–PpPh	#238	5						
Num–Pti	#239	2						
Num–PpPh	#240	8						
PpPh–Ni	#241	6						
PpPh–N<Ct>Ni	#242	4						
PpPh–PpPh	#243	3						
Totals 462		407	39		8		7	1

Table 10
Coordinate Declarative Verbless Clauses, Nucleus <P–S> ##281-321

Core --->	P–S		P.–S.P		SS,P–SR		SS,P.–SR.P		PS,PR–S
Nucleus									
N<Ct>Np–Pr					#310	1	#318	1	
N<Ct>Nd–Pr					#311	1			
Ns–Pr	#300	1							
Pti–Pr	#281	1							
Ni–Pr	##282,301,302	10	#309	1	##312,316	3	#319	5	
N<Ct>Ni–Pr	#283	1			#313	1			
Num–Pr					#314	2			
Adv–Pr									#321*
PpPh–Pr			#304	1	##315,317	3	#320	2	
Pti–Np			#305	1					
Adv–Np	#284	1							
PpPh–Np	#285	14							
PpPh–N<Ct>Np	#286	1							
Ni–Nd	#287	1	#306	1					
Np–N<Ct>Nd	#303	1							
Num–N<Ct>Nd	#288	3							
N<Ct>Ni–Ns	#289	2							
Num–Ns	#290	20	#307	1					
PpPh–Ns	#291	4							
Ni–Ni	#292	1	#308	1					
Num–Ni	#293	3							
Adv–Ni	#294	1							
PpPh–Ni	#295	5							
PpPh–N<Ct>Ni	#296	2							
Adv–Num	#297	1							
PpPh–Num	#298	11							
Ni–IfPh	#299	1							
Totals 110		85		6		11		8	

Table 11

Subordinate Declarative Verbless Clauses, Nucleus <S–P>, ##322-367

Core --->	S–P		S.–P.S		P.S–.P		SS,SR–P	
Nucleus								
Pr–Pr	#322*						#360	1
Pr–Np	#323	25						
Pr–Nd	#324	2					#361	4
Pr–N<Ct>Nd	#325	1					#362	1
Pr–Ptd	#326	2					#363	3
Pr–Nom							#364	1
Pr–Ns	#327	4					#365	1
Pr–N<Ct>Ns	#328	1						
Pr–Pti	#329	19			#357	10		
Pr–Ni	#330*						#366	1
Pr–PpPh	#331	1					#367	1
Np–N<Ct>Np	#332	1						
Np–Nd	#333	1						
Np–Ptd	#334	1						
Np–Pti	#335	2			#358	4		
Np–PpPh	#336	1	#356	2				
N<Ct>Np–Ns	#337	1						
N<Ct>Np–PpPh	##338,352	3						
Nd–Ni	#339	2						
Nd–PpPh	##340,353	3						
N<Ct>Nd–Np	#354	1						
N<Ct>Nd–Ni	##341*,355	1						
N<Ct>Nd–PpPh	#342	1						
Ns–Ptd	#343	2						
Ns–Ni	#344*							
Ns–PpPh	#345	3						
N<Ct>Ns–Ni	#346	1						
N<Ct>Ns–PpPh	#347	3						
Ni–PpPh	#348	6						
N<Ct>Ni–Pti					#359	1		
N<Ct>Ni–Ni	#349	1						
N<Ct>Ni–PpPh	#350	3						
Num–PpPh	#351	1						
Totals 123		93		2		15		13

Table 12
Subordinate Declarative Verbless Clauses, Nucleus <P–S>, ##368-439

Core ---> Nucleus	P–S	P.–S.P	SS,P–SR	SS,P.–SR.P	PS,PR–S / P.–S.P.S
Pr–Pr	#368 1				
N<Ct>Np–Pr	#369 5	#408*	#432 1		
N<Ct>Nd–Pr	#370 1				
Ns–Pr	#371 9	#409 2			
N<Ct>Ns–Pr	#372 2				
Pti–Pr	#373 5	##410,429 8			
Ni–Pr	##374,375,402 47	##411,412 430 22	#433 1	#436 2	
N<Ct>Ni–Pr	##376,403 19	#413 9	#434 1		
PpPh–Pr	#377 2	#414 1	#435 4	#437 2	
Pti–Np	#378 2	#415 4			
Ni–Np	##379*,380 1	#416 2			
Ni–N<Ct>Np	##381*,382 1	#417 1			
PpPh–N<Ct>Np		#418 1			
Ns–Nd	#383 1				
Pti–Nd	#384*	#419 1			
Ni–Nd	##385,386,404* 2	##420,421 6			
N<Ct>Ni–Nd	#387 1				
Adv–Nd					#438 1
PpPh–Nd	##388,405 4				
Ni–N<Ct>Nd		#422 1			
PpPh–N<Ct>Nd	#389 1				
Np–Ns	#390 1				
Pti–Ns	#391*	#423*			
Ni–Ns	##392,393 4	##424,431 2			
N<Ct>Ni–Ns	#394 2				
Part–Ns	#395 1				
PpPh–Ns	#406 1	##425,426 3			#439 1
Ni–N<Ct>Ns	#396 2				
N<Ct>Np–Pti	#397 1				
PpPh–Ni	#407 1				
N<Ct>Np–N<Ct>Ni	#398 4				
Ni–N<Ct>Ni		#427*			
PpPh–N<Ct>Ni	#399 2				
Ni–IfPh	#400 1	#428 1			
PpPh–PpPh	#401 1				
Totals 202	125	64	7	4	2

Table 13
Nominalized Declarative Verbless Clauses

Nucleus \<S–P\> #440-459			Nucleus \<P–S\> #460-473		
Nucleus			**Nucleus**		
Pr–Ns	#440	1	Ns–Pr	#470	1
Pr–Pti	##441,442	130	Pti–Pr	#471	1
Pr–Ni	##443,444	6	Ni–Pr	#472	1
			Part–Pr	#473	3
Pr–Adv	#445	3			
Pr–PpPh	#446	6			
Np–Pti	##447,448	47			
			Adv–Np	#460	1
Np–PpPh	#449	1			
			Adv–N\<Ct\>Np	#461	1
N\<Ct\>Np–PpPh	#450	1			
			Adv–Nd	#462	1
Nd–PpPh	#451	1	PpPh–Nd	#463	7
N\<Ct\>Nd–Np	#452	2			
N\<Ct\>Nd–Pti	#453	1			
			PpPh–N\<Ct\>Nd	#464	1
			Np–Ns	#465	1
Ns–Pti	##454,455	4			
Ns–Ni	#456	1			
Ns–PpPh	#457	2			
Ni–PpPh	#458	2	PpPh–Ni	##466,467	9
N\<Ct\>Ni–PpPh	#459	1	PpPh–N\<Ct\>Ni	#468	5
			PpPh–Num	#469	1
Totals		209			33

N.B. There are no discontinuities or resumptives in nominalized clauses.

Table 14
Precative Verbless Clauses, ##474-501

Core --->	S–P	S.–P.S		P–S	P.–S.P
Nucleus			Nucleus		
			Pti–Pr		#493 6
			w+Pti–Pr		##499-501 (5)
			Pti–Np	#484 5	#494 1
			w+Pti–Np	#497 (1)	
Np–PpPh	#479 2				
			Pti–Nd	##485,486 2	#495 1
			w+Pti–Nd	#498 (1)	
			Pti–Nom	#487 1	
Ns–Pti	#474 6		Pti–Ns	#488 4	
w+Ns–Pti	#496 (2)				
Ns–PpPh	#475 9				
			PpPh–Ns	##489,492 2	
			Pti–N<Ct>Ns	#490 2	
			Pti–Pti	#491 11	
Ni–PpPh					
##476,480,481	9	#482 4			
N<Ct>Ni–PpPh					
#477	2				
Num–PpPh	#478 1	#483 1			
Totals	29	5		27	8
	(2)			(2)	(5)
		36			42

N.B. The numbers of coordinate clauses are in parentheses.

Table 15
Interrogative Verbless Clauses, ##502-555

Core --->	S–P		P–S	
Interrogative				
mĭ/ma–			##502-514	54
Coordinated	#515	2	##516-519	8
Adv	##520,523	5	#534	2
hă–	##521,522,532,533	6	##535-539,544-548	13
hălŏ'	##524-531	10	##540-542,549*-551*,552	4
hăkĭ			#543	1
Coordinated	##553,554	3	#555	1
Totals 109		26		83

Notes

Previous Study of the Verbless Clause

[1] C. Albrecht, "Die Wortstellung im hebräischen Nominalsatze," *Zeitschrift für die alttestamentliche Wissenschaft,* VII (1887), 218-24; VIII (1888), 249-63. Karl Oberhuber, "Zur Syntax des Richterbuches: Der einfache Nominalsatz und die sog. nominale Apposition," *Vetus Testamentum,* III (1953), pp. 2-45, represents no advance in methodology. Instead of recognizing a clause with sequence P–S as a distinct category with its own laws of distribution, Oberhuber describes it in terms of "inversion" of normal sequence for psychological reasons or, for example, under the "inverting power" of *kî* (p. 41).

[2] W. Gesenius, *Hebrew Grammar,* trans. A. E. Cowley (Oxford, 1910), p. 454.

[3] Carl Brockelmann, *Hebräische Syntax* (Neukirchen, 1956), pp. 24-25.

[4] Ronald J. Williams, *Hebrew Syntax: An Outline* (Toronto, 1967), p. 98. The method of proof by illustration, when the chosen illustrations are in fact atypical, leads to results in which what is stated as the rule is the exception, and what is stated as the exception is the rule.

[5] Paul Auvray, *Initiation à l'Hébreu biblique* (Tournai, 1955), pp. 24, 25, 27, 30.

[6] Samuel G. Green, *A Handbook to Old Testament Hebrew* (London, 1908), p. 149.

[7] *Ibid.,* p. 49.

[8] R. Laird Harris, *Introductory Hebrew Grammar* (Grand Rapids, 1955), p. 3.

[9] James Kennedy, *Introduction to Biblical Hebrew* (London, 1898), p. 30. A fairly accurate statement of the syntax of the predicate "adjective" is found also in C. T. Wood and H. C. O. Lanchester, *A Hebrew Grammar* (2nd ed., London, 1920), p. 31.

[10] *Gesenius's Hebrew Grammar* (London, n.d.), p. 229.

[11] A. B. Davidson, *An Introductory Hebrew Grammar* (24th ed., Revised by J. E. McFadyen; Edinburgh, 1932), p. 44. This remains in the 25th edition revised by John Mauchline (Edinburgh, 1962), p. 40.

[12] J. Weingreen, *A Practical Grammar for Classical Hebrew* (Oxford, 1939), p. 33.

The Present Investigation

[1] See, to begin with, John Lyons, *Introduction to Theoretical Linguistics* (Cambridge, 1968), where references to additional literature may be found.

Criticism of Previous Work

[1] C. Albrecht, *ZAW* VII (1887); VIII (1888).

[2] *Hebräische Syntax,* p. 10. Compare #42.

[3] Paul Joüon, *Grammaire de l'Hébreu biblique* (2nd ed., Rome, 1947), p. 468.

[4] On the present state of the question, see Lyons, *Theoretical Linguistics,* pp. 172-80.

[5] Robert E. Longacre, *The Notion of Sentence:* Georgetown Monograph XX (Georgetown, 1967).

[6] This feature is not provided for in Hockett's definition: "A sentence is a grammatical form which is not in construction with any other grammatical form: a constitute which is not a constituent" (Charles F. Hockett, *A Course in Modern Linguistics* [New York, 1958], p. 199).

[7] This bears some resemblance to Leonard Bloomfield's description of a sentence as a nonincluded or maximum form (*Language* [New York, 1933], p. 170). It tries to compensate for the limitations of an analytical approach (seen in Hockett's definition quoted in note 6) by emphasizing that the sentence is a structural as well as a functional entity.

[8] Edward Sapir, *Language* (New York, 1949), p. 35.

[9] Manfred Sandmann, *Subject and Predicate: A Contribution to the Theory of Syntax* (Edinburgh, 1954).

[10] For example: *Wayyō'mer lāhem ya'ăqob 'ahay mē'ayin 'attem; wayyō'mərū mēhārān 'anāhnū,* "And Jacob said to them, 'My brothers, *from where* [are] you?' And they said, *From Haran* (P) [are] we' " (Gen. 29:4).

[11] This is what Brockelmann does, *Hebräische Syntax,* p. 23. See also Albrecht in *ZAW,* p. 223.

[12] The similar clauses *'iš-ṭōb ze,* "he is a good man" (II Sam. 18:27), and *dām ze,* "this is blood" (II Kings 3:23), show that *ze* cannot mean "here." The statements answer the question "Who?" not "Where?" A similar clause in I Kings 20:41 has *hū'* for *ze.* Compare ##322 and 368.

[13] They are Gen. 7:2; 17:12; Num. 17:5; Deut. 17:15; 20:15.

[14] Oskar Grether, *Hebräische Grammatik für den akademischen Unterricht* (2nd ed., München, 1955), p. 229. The example seems to have been copied from Albrecht (p. 220). Similar objections apply to the summary of the syntax of the nominal sentence by Beer (*Hebräische Grammatik,* rev. Rudolf Meyer [2nd ed., Berlin, 1955], II, 94-96). Examples are given which do not represent statistically predominant constructions; others are invalid because they omit part of the sentence or ignore the context.

[15] Albrecht, p. 259.

[16] The analysis of Otto Eissfeldt, *Hexateuch-Synopse* (Leipzig, 1922), has been taken as standard. Besides the usual J (and L), E, D, and P, the Book of the Covenant (C) and the Holiness Code (H) are distinguished. There is no need to indicate D for most of Deuteronomy.

A Linguistic Model: The Tagmeme and the Syntagmeme

[1] A generalized theory of the syntagmeme was presented in this author's (unpublished) doctoral dissertation "Studies in Hebrew Syntax," 1960.

[2] *International Journal of American Linguistics,* XXIV (1958), 273-78.

[3] For theoretical developments somewhat parallel to those of the present writer, see Robert E. Longacre, "Some Fundamental Insights of Tagmemics," *Language,* XLI, (1965), 65-76.

[4] Benjamin Elson and Velma B. Pickett, *An Introduction to Morphology and Syntax* (Santa Ana, 1964), p. 57.

[5] Robert E. Longacre, "String Constituent Analysis," *Language,* XXXVI (1960), 63-68; *Grammar Discovery Procedures:* Janua Linguarum, series minor No. 33 (The Hague, 1964).

[6] Velma B. Pickett, *An Introduction to the Study of Grammatical Structure* (Glendale, 1956).

[7] Benjamin Elson, *Beginning Morphology-Syntax* (Glendale, 1960).

[8] Velma B. Pickett, *The Grammatical Hierarchy of Isthmus Zapotec:* Language Dissertation No. 56, Supplement to *Language,* XXXVI (1960); Viola Waterhouse, *The Grammatical Structure of Oaxaca Chontal:* Publication Nineteen of the Indiana University Research Center in Anthropology, Folklore, and Linguistics, *International Journal of American Linguistics,* XXVIII (1962).

[9] Robert E. Longacre, "From Tagma to Tagmeme in Biblical Hebrew," *A William Cameron Townsend en el vigésimoquinto aniversario del Instituto Lingüístico de Verano* (México, D.F., 1961), pp. 563-91.

[10] Elson and Pickett (note 4), p. 62. Compare: "The formal signals of structural meanings operate in a system—that is, . . . the items of form and arrangement have signaling significance only as they are parts of patterns in a structural whole" (Charles C. Fries, *The Structure of English* [New York, 1952], pp. 59-60).

[11] See Lyons, p. 155.

[12] For literature see the contributions of Noam Chomsky and George A. Miller to *Handbook of Mathematical Psychology,* II, R. Duncan Luce, Robert R. Bush, and Eugene Galanter, eds. (New York, 1963).

[13] Ferdinand de Saussure, *Cours de linguistique génerale* (5th ed., Paris, 1955).

[14] See C. E. Bazell, "On the Problem of the Morpheme," *Archivum Linguisticum*, I (1949), 1-20 for a discussion of the difficulty of analyzing such constructions.

[15] L. V. Shcherba, "Ocheredniye problemy yazykovvedeniya," *Izvestiya Akademii nauk S.S.S.R.: Otdeleniye literatury i yazyka*, IV (1945).

[16] A. A. Reformatskiĭ, *Vvedeniye v yazykoznaniye* (2nd ed., Moscow, 1955), 253, note 1. In the fourth edition of this work (*Vvedeniye v yazykovedeniye* [Moscow, 1967]) the concept of *syntagma* is applied with more grammatical precision and with wider scope. The extension to sentence-level constructions resembles in some respects the method developed independently by this author. See especially pp. 325-27, 335-37.

[17] Louis Hjelmslev, *Prolegomena to a Theory of Language:* Indiana University Publications in Anthropology and Linguistics, Memoir VII of the *International Journal of American Linguistics* (1953).

[18] Kenneth L. Pike, *Language*, Part III (1st ed., Glendale, 1960), p. 1. The question of focus on function or relationship is explored in Chapter 11 of the second edition (1967).

[19] This terminology is used by Viola Waterhouse, *The Grammatical Structure of Oaxaca Chontal*.

Grammatical Constructions and Relationships in the Verbless Clause

[1] w^e– (or w) stands for all its allomorphs.

[2] Hockett, *Modern Linguistics*, p. 184.

Precative Clauses

[1] On the language of "blessing" see W. Sibley Towner, "Blessed be Yahweh" *Catholic Biblical Quarterly*, XXX (1968), 386-99.

Interrogative Clauses

[1] Sometimes, however, it seems as if the normal sequence may be inverted to bring the item on which the question is focused nearer the interrogator. Compare Judg. 15:2 and I Sam. 1:8 with I Sam. 9:21.

Rules and Exceptions

[1] H. A. Gleason, *An Introduction to Descriptive Linguistics* (New York, 1955), pp. 145-46.

[2] M. Dahood, *Psalms I:* Anchor Bible (New York, 1966), pp. xxxvii, 17, 45, 114; *Psalms II:* Anchor Bible (New York, 1968), p. 282. By the same token, the clauses in #24 announce divine names.

[3] For a discussion of a similar construction in the *Meša'* Inscription see *Orientalia*, XXXV (1966), p. 107.

[4] The author has worked this out in *Ibid.*, p. 107.

[5] Equating Hebrew *'imrē-šāper* with Akkadian *immir-supūri*.

[6] The key to the new interpretation is the rejection of the difficult *grm*, "bone," by recognizing *gr*, "sojourn," plus enclitic *mem*. Revocalization of *ḥmr* to *nomen professionis* **ḥammāru* is due to Dr. W. F. Albright, who also makes *mrbṣ* a participle (*Yahweh and the Gods of Canaan* [New York, 1968], p. 266). Identification of *ben hammišp^etayim* or the like (compare Ps. 68:14) as "smith," literally "son(s) of the bellows," secures synonymous parallelism in line with parallels X || ben–Y throughout Gen. 49.

[7] W. F. Albright, *Ibid.*, p. 13.

[8] "An Interpretation of the Akkadian Stative as a Nominal Sentence" *Journal of Near Eastern Studies*, XXVII (1968), 1-12. Nonverbal clause patterns in Egyptian also offer important typological comparisons with Semitic; compare Sarah Israelit Groll, *Nonverbal Sentence Patterns in Late Egyptian* (London, 1967).

[9] Herbert B. Huffmon, *Amorite Personal Names in the Mari Texts* (Baltimore, 1965), pp. 95-96.

[10] Wolfram von Soden, *Grundriss der akkadischen Grammatik* (Rome, 1962), ##126-27.

[11] D. J. Wiseman, *The Alalakh Tablets* (London, 1953), p. 33; AT *6:21-24. Improved text thanks to Dr. Anne Kilmer.

[12] E. A. Speiser, *Genesis:* Anchor Bible (New York, 1964), p. 355.

[13] *wm-* plus a perfect verb may be recognized also in *wmpl'* (Judg. 13:19) and *wmsrpw* (Amos 6:10), the participles being otherwise unknown. This clears up Ruth 4:5, where the difficulty of *wm't* is reflected in the versions. There is no need to normalize to verse 10 (*w*ᵉ*gam 'et-rūt* . . .), following Vulgate and Syriac. LXX supports MT as an ancient reading. A literal translation, with *min-*, misses the point: the field is not to be acquired *from* Ruth as well as from Naomi; rather, when the field is acquired from Naomi, Ruth must be acquired with it, and is the object of the following verb. Other examples of enclitic *mem* with *w-* may be present in II Sam. 16:5; Job 6:22; 7:14; 10:14; 19:26; 21:20.

[14] Albrecht cites Num. 14:3 to show that P-S is an exception to his main rule (p. 221), connecting the supposed abnormality with interrogation. But the sequence is normal.

[15] In contrast to Albrecht, who thinks that S-P is the rule for everything, Joüon gives <PpPh-S> as the normal sequence (*Grammaire de l'Hébreu biblique*, p. 469).

The Presentation of the Evidence in the Corpus

[1] On the special problem of #515 see pp. 38-39.

Index